DRIP SYSTEM WATERING

ALSO BY JACK KRAMER

One Thousand Beautiful House Plants & How to Grow Them
Cacti & Other Succulents
Your Homemade Greenhouse & How to Build It
Your Trellis Garden: How to Build It, How to Grow It, How to Show It
The Old-Fashioned Cutting Garden
Growing Orchids at Your Window
Plant Language
The Log House Book

DRIP SYSTEM WATERING

FOR BIGGER AND BETTER PLANTS

by Jack Kramer

W · W · NORTON & COMPANY · *NEW YORK* · *LONDON*

FIRST EDITION

THIS TEXT is composed in photocomposition Baskerville. The display type used is handset Bauer Weiss. Manufacturing is by the Maple-Vail Book Manufacturing Group. Book design by Marjorie J. Flock.

The following drawings are by Carol Carlson: Water absorption; How plants use water; Flower garden, house plant, and vegetable garden irrigation; Mini system drip irrigation; Self-watering tray; and Patio drip system.
Other drawings by Michael Valdez.

Library of Congress Cataloging in Publication Data
Kramer, Jack, 1927–
    Drip system watering for bigger and better plants.
    1. Trickle irrigation. 2. Gardening. I. Title.
S619.T74K7 1980   635'.04'87   79–17372

ISBN 0-393-01299-9

1 2 3 4 5 6 7 8 9 0

Contents

Contents   6

Preface

TODAY THERE ARE over eight million home gardens, but the majority of gardeners are not growing plants properly. There is a great deal of money unnecessarily wasted in cultivating plants. Water—the lifeline of a plant—and how you water plants and how much, are the keys to successful gardening; if you are watering with a hose or sprinklers you are not getting half the produce from your vegetables or fruits, nor are you getting a tenth of the growth from your ornamental gardens. A new system of watering called drip irrigation takes the guesswork out of where and how much to water, and gives you a garden with robust plants, beautiful flowers, and a rewarding harvest of food plants.

Drip system gardening is the process of applying small amounts of water to plants at frequent intervals. It can be an elaborate system you buy (still not expensive), or a homemade system you can make. Drip irrigation saves water, of course, and saves you time (you can water your garden in about fifteen minutes). More important, by putting water where it is needed (at plant roots) your plants grow faster and more uniformly than with sprinkler watering for example. Drip systems also eliminate the problem of drainage, which most gardeners have in providing for their plants.

In this book we show and tell you how to set up a drip irrigation system for your garden—no matter what kind it is, no matter how large or small. We give exact charts of water absorption and penetration, and detailed working drawings that enable you to set up your drip watering system for fruit and vegetable gardens, ornamental gardens, for trees and shrubs. And even for container gardens.

If you want to grow plants properly (and who doesn't), and if you want a lot of flowers or a bountiful food harvest or bigger and better trees and shrubs, try this new way of successful gardening with drip watering systems. It is the wave of the future in gardening and now is the time to jump right in and have the biggest, best, and healthiest garden in your neighborhood.

J. J. K.

Acknowledgments

I WISH TO EXPRESS my thanks to the many manufacturers and suppliers of drip system watering who gave freely of their information and time in the preparation of this book. Special thanks go to Bob Anthis of Care-Free Irrigation Supplies of San Juan Capistrano, California, who made his notes and knowledge available to me, and to Rose Marie Christy of Sub Terrain Irrigation Systems of Santa Ana, California, who allowed us to use materials from her brochures, especially information from "Drip Irrigation for Landscaping and Gardens" by Bob Randall.

DRIP SYSTEM WATERING

1. Why Drip Watering?

IF YOU ARE WATERING your plants with conventional hoses or sprinklers—even with underground sprinkler systems—you are not really watering your plants. You are watering the ground—because only a minute percentage of water from sprinklers and hoses reaches plant roots. The result: you waste water, waste money, and your plants never really grow—they merely exist.

Water determines whether a plant grows or dies, and it is not so much a question of when to water plants as how much water to give plants. Most gardeners overwater plants and waste water by using conventional methods of watering, such as by hoses and sprinklers. However, by applying a specified amount of water *slowly* to plants' roots, as is done in drip systems, you contribute to the overall well-being of plants, without overdoing the amount of water you give them. Let's prove this by looking at some conventional watering methods.

Watering with Hoses

It takes water from a hose 1½ hours to penetrate 24 inches into the soil. Because most plants (trees and shrubs especially) have roots far below the surface of the soil and roots must get water in order for plants to grow, you would have to hose almost all day before the moisture reached deep into the soil to the plants' roots. And in the process you waste water. Water from a hose moves laterally in the soil; it does not fan out to any degree. Consider the penetration times shown in Table 1.

TABLE 1/TIME FOR WATER TO PENETRATE SOILS (*minutes*)

	Types of soil		
Soil depth	Coarse sand	Sandy loam	Clay loam
12 inches	15	30	60
24 inches		60	
30 inches	40		
48 inches	60		

Hoses are made of a number of materials; my hardware store stocks six different kinds. Many of the hoses crack or craze in cold weather or lose resiliency after a time. Rubber hoses last a long time and do not crack, but they are expensive (from $30 to $50). If you have even a small garden you would need two, possibly three hoses. You can install a drip watering system at almost the same cost and save water as you save your plants.

Incidentally, watering with a hose results in spotty watering, that is, there will be pockets of wet and dry soil. Not all the roots receive water, and so they grow in other directions, seeking moisture. This saps strength from your plants. Always remember that water moves laterally.

Water absorption

CONVENTIONAL WATERING

WET SOIL

DRY SOIL

DRIP WATERING

WET SOIL

DRY SOIL

Water penetration

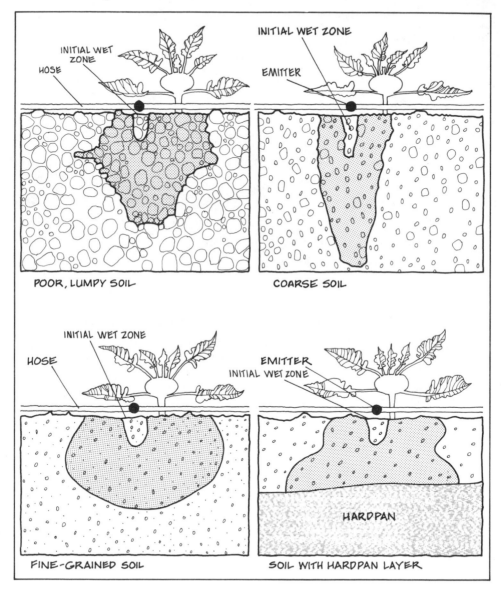

POOR, LUMPY SOIL

COARSE SOIL

FINE-GRAINED SOIL

SOIL WITH HARDPAN LAYER

Watering with Sprinklers

In recent years sprinklers have become very sophisticated. Suppliers carry more than a dozen different kinds. There are sprinklers that send water to and fro (oscillating), sprinklers that send water in an arc or circle, some that pulsate water, and some that simply spew water in all directions. There are also sprinkler systems that can be installed in the ground; they turn on at the flick of a switch (or without a switch) and are regulated by a time clock. Sprinklers may be fine in rare situations (and very costly as well), but they do a poor job of delivering water to plant roots.

Portable / Permanent Sprinklers

Portable sprinklers invariably have to be moved at different times to different areas (unless you purchase several of them), and generally can only deliver water to a 7- to 9-foot radius. Permanent buried sprinkler systems deliver water to an overall area—they water everything, not only the plants that need moisture. In other words, water falls away from the plant rather than on it. Most of the water evaporates in the air and runs off the surface of the soil, especially in clay or hard soil. Also, what if you change your plantings, as so often happens in a garden? Either you must move portable sprinklers about or revamp an underground permanent system. Many sprinklers break down after a short time, and although some may do a better job than others, most sprinklers waste water.

Finally, as the water pressure fluctuates within the sprinkler—and it does—the area moistened receives erratic watering. To prove that sprinklers are vastly over-

Sprinklers, no matter what kind, send water into the air on everything and anything, rather than putting moisture at plant roots where it is needed.   *Photo courtesy U.S.D.A.*

In an effort to keep crops growing, man has tried many methods of irrigation. This pipe flood system delivers water to plant roots—the main prerequisite for good plant growth. *Photo courtesy U.S.D.A.*

Sprinklers such as these may be satisfactory for large commercial fields, but for home gardens the drip system is the answer to watering.   *Photo courtesy U.S.D.A.*

rated, set an empty can in the area of your plants, turn on the sprinklers, and note how long it takes (hours) for the can to fill up with water.

Irrigation

Crops and plants, whether on small farms or giant agri-business complexes, in home gardens small or large, must have water in order to grow. Yet it is estimated that by the year 2000, 20 to 25 percent of this country's stream flow will be depleted (stream flow is our major source of water; only 2 percent of our water comes from wells). Already many areas of the southwestern United States, areas that have an adequate surface water flow, have had their underground water supplies so heavily tapped that the supplies are exhausted, with no hope of replacement.

Another problem, especially in parts of the West, has been lack of sufficient snowfall in the mountains. As snow melts, it runs down mountains and into streams, but without this runoff and rainfall, the streams cannot replenish themselves. Also, two-fifths of our land mass (e.g., California, Arizona, and Texas) is considered arid, with less than 20 inches of rain annually.

The main methods of irrigation (watering)—sprinkler and drip—have been developed to meet the needs of different areas and crops, based on the principles of soil management and cost. The same factors must be considered with regard to home gardens: (1) cost of the water; (2) slope of the ground; (3) texture of the soil; (4) type of plant grown; (5) the availability, quantity, and quality of the water; (6) other problems such as salinity and poor drainage. And of course, local weather conditions must be taken into account as well.

Cost of the Water

The cost of water is no longer minimal in most areas—using excessive water for gardens can run into many dollars. Consult your local water company to determine water rates, and then check your water meter after a day of routine watering to find out exactly what you are paying for upkeep of the area. You might be surprised to learn what you are spending on water.

Good evidence of water cost occurred in the drought years of 1976 and 1977 in California, when water was about six cents per gallon. This, of course, is exorbitant—yet the time may come when water is this costly. Thus a drip system saving as much as 60 percent in water cost makes good sense.

Slope of the Ground

If you have ever hose- or sprinkler-watered a hillside, you know that 90 percent of the water is wasted because it runs downhill into gutters and ditches, and so plants are in danger of perishing from lack of moisture. However, if you use drip systems and emitters in strategic places, water does reach plant roots, with little or none wasted, and plants grow and grow.

The practical answer for plants on slopes or terraced gardens, without doubt, is a drip system. It not only saves valuable dollars, it saves the plants and is the only way really to have a handsome garden without the constant chore of daily watering.

Texture of the Soil

Soil texture (tilth) is vital to plant health and also affects the way in which you water. Soil must be porous so that water can flow through it. How quickly and thoroughly

Watering a home garden slope such as this presents a problem because with conventional watering, most of the moisture runs off. Again, a drip watering setup is the answer. *Photo courtesy Sub Terrain Irrigation Co.*

A closeup showing pipes in place on slope garden.   *Photo courtesy Sub Terrain Irrigation Co.*

water reaches plant roots depends on the soil texture—in sandy soils water runs through quickly, whereas in clay soils water has a tough time penetrating the soil. If you have reasonably porous soil, a standard emitter setup (as explained in Chapter 5) is fine, but if the soil is hard, you may need more emitters to cover given areas of plantings.

To determine if your soil is sandy or clayey, dig up a spadeful and run it through your hands. It should feel porous and mealy, like a well-done baked potato. If soil is claylike, there are products on the market to break up the clay. The easiest way is to rototill the soil to ensure good porosity.

Type of Plants Grown

It is prudent to evaluate what type of plants you are growing before you determine the type of drip system to install. Vegetable gardens will need more water more often than, say, an ornamental garden of shrubs and trees. Vegetables grow quickly and use up water quickly, as do flower gardens. A garden composed only of evergreens, however, can maintain itself on less water than the flower garden.

Plan your garden first as to plants and then decide on the specific drip system for it (see Chapter 4).

Other Factors

Other factors when considering a drip system are the quality and availability of water. Obviously, in areas where water is in short supply a drip system is almost essential, and if the water is saline (which is harmful to most plants), drip systems are also called for. With regular watering saline water—it is too salty—can kill plants, but with drip watering, which administers small amounts slowly, the salinity is diluted to a safe level.

2. Water—Plants' Lifeline

THE GREATER PART of a plant—the roots—is below ground. The roots do the work: they pull up the water that is necessary for photosynthesis, the process whereby the sun helps the plant to manufacture food. A constant supply of water, in just the right amounts, is what makes plants really grow. To understand how to water your plants successfully with a drip watering system, it is necessary to know a little about how a plant grows.

Plant Parts

First, plants consist of roots, stems, leaves, flowers, fruits, and seeds; these organs all work together. The function of the roots is to hold plants in the ground and to absorb water and necessary chemical substances. Some roots are long and tapered, shaped like a carrot. Other plants have fat roots that store food; and corms, rhizomes, and bulbs have short feeding roots that gather moisture and food. Grass roots are shallow because they gather food just below the surface of the soil, whereas the roots of a large tree branch out into an enormous network to grip the soil and hold the tree in place.

There is a relationship between the total leaf surface exposed to the sun and the total root surface in contact with the soil. If water is not available to the roots, a plant dies. Root tips are made of tough flat cells that push forward from pressure exerted by the plant growth behind them. The tips squeeze and force their way through the ground, surmounting all obstacles. Behind the root tip or cone is the growing area of the root, which contains the young cells that multiply by dividing in two. As the plant develops, so do the roots. Main roots send out smaller ones, which in turn also develop roots. The older roots become tubes that carry the water and nutrients to the plant, or sometimes act as storage reservoirs for food. Roots also develop delicate hairs that perform the actual absorption of water and food. The tiny hairs are sensitive to light and dryness, shriveling and dying quickly when exposed to air. Roots cannot grow upward; root growth is a downward curve.

Stems and trunks store, distribute, and process the products of leaves and roots of nearly all plants. Each cell in a stem must have a constant supply of moisture, food, and air, and must also store food for emergencies. A stem manufactures and processes as well as stores and handles distribution and transportation of food. As growth begins in a plant, a central stem (or group of stems) develops and pushes up from the ground as it seeks light. The growth tip of the seed forms the stem. The stem carries on the functions of the roots and root hairs of transporting water and nutrients to buds, leaves, and flowers, and it returns the sugars manufactured in the leaves to the roots. The stem also supports the plant and can be rigid or flexible. The stem is essentially the conveyor pipe that moves the sugars from the leaves to the roots, where the sugars are stored as starch.

How plants use water

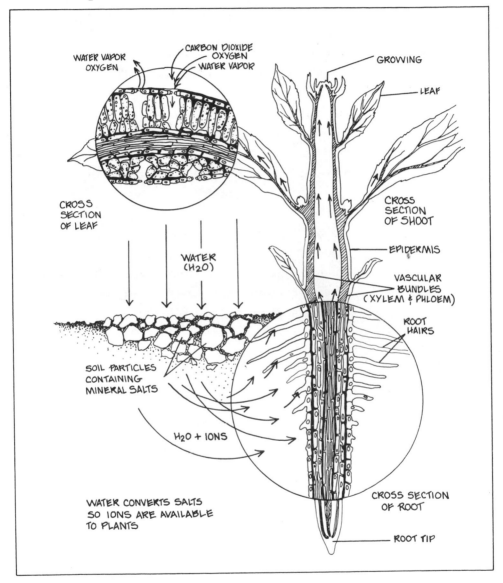

WATER VAPOR
OXYGEN

CARBON DIOXIDE
OXYGEN
WATER VAPOR

GROWING

LEAF

CROSS
SECTION
OF LEAF

CROSS
SECTION
OF SHOOT

EPIDERMIS

WATER
(H₂O)

VASCULAR
BUNDLES
(XYLEM & PHLOEM)

ROOT
HAIRS

SOIL PARTICLES
CONTAINING
MINERAL SALTS

H₂O + IONS

CROSS SECTION
OF ROOT

WATER CONVERTS SALTS
SO IONS ARE AVAILABLE
TO PLANTS

ROOT TIP

The leaves make organic food out of sunlight, air, water, and earth salts. In other words, most of the carbohydrates required by a plant are manufactured in the leaves by the process of photosynthesis. The energy of the sun is changed into a form that can be used in the life process of a plant. This process depends on chlorophyll, the green material in plants. Photosynthesis takes carbon dioxide, water, and the energy of the sun, and produces carbohydrates and sugar.

The entire process of a leaf is to combine gas and liquid. In one form or another a leaf obtains oxygen, hydrogen, carbon, and nitrogen, along with other elements. Water supplies the hydrogen and oxygen; carbon comes to the roots through the humus in the earth. Nitrogen is vital to the plant, but it can be used only in liquid form. Another leaf activity is transpiration, or the emitting of water as vapor. When plants cannot get moisture, their leaves wilt and shrivel, and eventually the plants die.

Flowers and Fruits

Plants reproduce and perpetuate themselves through the production of seeds. The flower contains the female parts that, when fertilized with male sexual cells, produce seed. The seed holds a plant's life for an indefinite time until the right conditions occur to start the seed growing.

How Plants Grow

Plants' growth depends on air, light, nutrients in the soil, temperature, water, and type of soil. When these conditions are at optimum levels, plants thrive; but rarely is there a precise balance of these factors, so we must help provide the balance—including watering.

A good circulation of air keeps plants healthy. Crowded conditions rob plants of light, and dusty and smoggy air hinders plants' growth by blocking the air pores and cells. And the rate of water loss from a plant is influenced by the relative humidity of the air: the drier the air, the more water lost. If water loss is too great, the plant withers. Wind increases the rate of water loss, modifies the water content of plant cells, and affects the form of growth of plants.

Light affects photosynthesis and the synthesis of chlorophyll as well as the temperature of a plant (most of the light that strikes plants' foliage is changed to heat, thus raising the plants' temperatures). The form and growth of leaves are also controlled by light; plants with thick leaves like sun, and those that grow in shade generally have thin leaves.

The three most important elements in plants' diets are nitrogen, phosphorus, and potassium; some trace elements are also required. Nitrogen promotes leaf growth, phosphorus promotes root and stem development, and potash (containing usable potassium) stabilizes growth and intensifies color. These foods must be in the soil if plants are to maintain proper health. The lack of any one of these elements halts plants' normal growth and development. Temperature influences every process that goes on in a plant: photosynthesis, assimilation, digestion, respiration, water absorption, transpiration, and the formation of enzymes.

An adequate supply of water is necessary if plants are to do their best. When all other conditions are good, plants can consume a great deal of water. The way in which roots absorb water, and how much, depends on the soil. Growers have to know the water-storage capacity of the soil (the place where the roots are situated) and the rate of water used by the plants. Just how much water the soil can store is determined mostly by the soil's texture (tilth), the size of the soil's particles, and their distribution. For example, a fine-textured soil such as clay can hold about twice as much water as a sandy soil.

TABLE 2/WATER STORAGE IN SOIL

Soil texture	Available water per foot of soil depth (inches)	Gallons per cubic foot of soil
Sand	½ to 1	⅓ to ⅔
Sandy loam	1 to 1½	⅔ to 1
Clay loam	¼ to ½	½ to ⅔
Clay	⅛ to ¼	¼ to ½

As Table 2 shows, 1 inch of water is the amount that would cover the surface of soil 1 inch deep; 1½ inches covering 1 square foot equals 1 gallon.

The water-storage capacity of soil also depends on how deep the plant roots penetrate. If there is normal moisture in the soil, the top 3 or 4 feet is considered the water-storage tank for most trees and shrubs. In dry periods those deep-rooted plants will draw water from farther down.

How Plants Use Water

Most of the water that plants receive goes out through their leaves as water vapor and evaporates from the soil. This process is known as evapotranspiration (abbreviated ET). The rate of ET is influenced by the climate, the sun, temperature, humidity, and wind. Drip irrigation is based on the water-storage capacity of the soil and the ET rate. Growers watch for such symptoms of moisture need in plants as wilting of leaves, change of appearance in leaves, shiny leaves becoming dull, bright-green leaves fading to gray-green, and leaves falling off the plant. The growers also check by rolling a small amount of soil into a ball. If the soil does not form a ball, it is too dry; if the soil molds into a ball but does not crumble when you rub it with your finger, the soil is too wet. Growers have to be careful not to overirrigate because too much water can be bad for plants. The idea is to use just enough water to fill up the water-storage reservoir, wait until plants have used up half that water, and then add more.

If you are watering in small amounts, plant roots get little if any moisture because the water is wasted through direct evaporation from the soil. Too frequent shallow moisture also encourages shallow rooting and may cause root rot and other diseases. You have to know how fast water is being applied through your pipes in order to know the right amount of water to apply. This is easy if your water is metered. If it is not, put six to eight cans in a circular pattern to measure the rate of application in inches per hour.

Thus, there is more to watering plants and how plants use water effectively than meets the eye. A perfect balance of all requirements is what the average gardener strives for, and it is far easier to reach that perfection using drip watering than using conventional systems. In essence, drip watering provides you with a satisfactory means of meeting plants' needs so they grow big and beautiful.

3. Introduction to Drip Watering

THE BASIC IDEA of drip irrigation came into use in Germany about 1860–1870. Clay pipes with open joints were laid beneath the surface of the soil; water was applied gradually to crops as the water table rose and fell during the year. In the following decades, little was done to utilize this first attempt at drip watering, but finally in the 1930s the Australians, out of necessity, devised a watering system for peach orchards using galvanized iron pipes with holes cut in them. Water is a scarce item in Australia, so conserving it while still using it to produce food was a crucial need.

In 1948 greenhouse growers in England successfully tried drip watering for tomatoes. In 1960, drip irrigation techniques were first used in the United States. Orchards in particular were testing grounds, and later drip irrigation was extended to the growing of tomatoes, grapes, strawberries, corn, and other crops.

Much earlier, Smycah Blass of Israel devised a system that had a coiled emitter which would not clog. The emitter was a spiral tube in a hard casing; the tube reduced the discharge pressure by lengthening the flow path of the water—hence it was possible to discharge water through a larger hole. The Blass system of drip irrigation was used in Israel with great success. Furrow and sprinkler systems had produced poor yields, but drip watering yielded a large and healthy bounty. The key to success in this application was that drip irrigation can generally utilize highly saline water, such as that found in the deserts of Israel.

From these commercial beginnings, drip watering has evolved into an efficient and proven method for producing better and bigger plants in home gardens as well. In Chapter 4 we will explore all the ways of using this concept for the home grounds.

Drip Irrigation—For All Plants and Seeds?

Can you use drip systems for all plants—shrubs, trees, perennials, annuals, fruit trees, and ground covers? Yes! Trees and shrubs will grow faster and better, flowers will be larger and greater in number, fruit trees will produce bigger and better fruit, and ground covers will spread more quickly.

In other words, a drip system in one form or another is the basic answer to the worry-free and productive garden because it supplies almost total watering.

If you are starting plants from seed—vegetables, for example—drip watering by a regulated soaker system is an excellent way of getting a heavy harvest. Applied moisture at a slow, constant rate is exactly what seeds require to germinate and grow. The regulated-pressure soaker system is different from a soaker hose (a hose with holes in it; more detail about this appears in a later chapter). Soaker pressure systems installed un-

An above-ground system of drip watering; note the emitter (placed exactly at plant roots) and wet areas. *Photo courtesy Sub Terrain Irrigation Co.*

Underground systems eliminate the need for pipes on the surface; the line is buried 3 inches below soil and only the emitter (at left) shows. *Photo courtesy Drip and Mist Watering Co.*

This underground drip system waters foundation plantings. The tiny emitter does the job. *Photo courtesy Drip and Mist Watering Co.*

This closeup photo shows that the root zone area is wet. Water is put where the plant can really use it. The emitter is hidden behind the plant. *Photo courtesy Drip and Mist Watering Co.*

derground enable you to pick vegetables while they are being watered. The constant flow of water to seeds enables them to germinate more quickly than with spotty hose watering, and keeps them growing rapidly. Vegetables are greedy, and even the most dedicated gardener may forget to put the hose on now and then, but with drip soaker systems water is applied to plants with the flick of the wrist and in predetermined amounts—not too much, never too little. Remember that seed beds which go dry even for a day can result in a ruined crop in your backyard.

If you are growing roses, a drip system of watering will eliminate that fungal nemesis that develops on foliage when kept too wet. Sprinklers invariably wet the leaves—drip watering does not, so there is a big plus here. In addition, your crop of flowers will be doubled.

Hanging baskets and potted plants of any kind on a patio or terrace will benefit greatly when grown with a drip watering setup. Growth is rapid and plants flourish—mine do. And even indoors a small drip setup can be installed to water your house plants and keep them beautiful. If plants are grouped in one area—and generally they are—the drip concept of watering works well indoors too. (See Chapter 6.)

Drip watering is a boon for fruit trees because with this method trees really bear; again, watering slowly and steadily does the job. And if you have a lawn there is even a drip system that will keep it lush and green (see Chapter 4).

Advantages

There are endless advantages to drip irrigation. For one thing, there is less surface soil but more root area soil wetted by drip irrigation than by other irrigation methods. Agricultural researchers and experienced gardeners believe that at least 33 percent of the soil in the root zone of mature crops must be wetted for peak growth and that crop performance improves as the amount of root soil wetted increases to 60 percent or more.

Frequent drip irrigation maintains an evenly moist root soil, one that does not fluctuate between wet and dry extremes. It keeps most of the root soil well aerated. Another plus is that there is less drying time between irrigations; salts in the root soil water are kept more diluted and thus a saltier water can be applied than by using other watering methods without causing damage to the plants.

Weed growth is reduced by drip irrigation because only the root, rather than the surface soil, is wetted. And drip irrigation dispenses water slowly, closer to the rate at which the root soil can absorb it. Water then flows by capillary action into the soil; the soil is not drowned as it is with standard watering practices. This slow absorption via frequent watering provides steady moisture for and plants, causing many plants to grow bigger and better. This is especially true on slopes because there is much less runoff. And with a drip system there is no need to create basins around plants and trees—a time-consuming job—to hold water.

The drip system is easy to automate; it can be controlled by automatic valves and moisture-sensing emitters, timing devices, and so on. You can even install a fertilizer injector into the system; this injector puts the nutrients in their correctly diluted form right into the root area. You also save water with drip irrigation systems because no water is lost by evaporation in the air (since the water is down in the root area). This form of irrigation can save as much as 40 to 60 percent on water compared with conventional watering methods.

By using less water and having the capability of being automated, the drip irrigation system can thus save you time and money. You do not have to spend as much time watering and pulling weeds, and applying fertilizers, and since you will be using less water you will decrease your water bills. Also, a drip system can be buried or left on the surface of the ground. When buried, the system cannot be vandalized and is not conspicuous in the landscape.

The system is good on the surface for flower and vegetable gardens because it can be moved out of the way when you are cultivating the flowers and crops. In addition, a drip system is ideally suited for those potted and hanging plants that normally are hard to water. And if you grow roses, as mentioned you will have less mildew on the plants because the system will wet only the roots, not the foliage.

The drip system slows the flow of water by reducing its pressure. Water is pumped to homes in most districts at pressures ranging from 50 to 90 pounds per square inch (psi). Drip systems usually deliver water to your plants at pressures ranging from 2 to 45 psi. The systems have either a regulator or a pressure-dissipating device in the emitters and some kind of screen or filter to keep the emitters from becoming clogged with soil.

Complete drip irrigation systems with emitters, hoses, pressure reducers, and filters are available for both small and large gardens. The prices of the drip systems vary (see Chapter 5), and they can be purchased at discount houses, nurseries, hardware stores, and through magazine ads. There are also several mail-order suppliers.

Disadvantages

Drip systems for gardens, good as they are, should not be considered miracle workers. Things can and do go wrong with some systems—and some technical aptitude and knowledge is necessary to install a watering setup.

Because the emitter outlets are very small, they can become clogged by particles of minerals or organic matter. This clogging can reduce the emission rate of water and upset the uniformity of water distribution, thus causing plant damage. In some cases, particles present in the irrigation water are not adequately filtered out, or particles may form in the water as the water stands in the lines or evaporates from emitter holes between irrigations. Iron oxide, calcium carbonate, algae, and microbial slimes may form in drip irrigation systems in certain locations. Phosphate fertilizers in irrigation waters can also cause clogging because phosphate reacts with any calcium in the water, forming a precipitate that can clog fine-mesh filters and emitters. Fortunately, chemical treatment of the water can prevent or correct most of these emitter-clogging problems; self-flushing emitters are the other answer.

Many emitters operate at low pressures, 2 to 20 psi. If an area slopes steeply, the nozzle discharge during irrigation may differ up to 50 percent from that intended, and the lines may drain through lower emitters after the water is shut off. Thus, some plants receive too much water and others receive too little. However, this can be remedied with pressure-compensating emitters.

Some soils may not have sufficient capacity to absorb water that is being dripped at the standard discharge rate. If so, runoff or undesirable ponding (or puddling) occurs. For example, if water is being discharged at a rate of 1 gallon per hour (gph), the soil must have an absorption capacity of 0.5 inches per hour of water to keep the pool of free water around the emitter from exceeding 2 feet in diameter. Sandy soils are probably best adapted to drip irrigation, especially those with slight horizontal stratification. Such stratification is beneficial for drip irrigation because it promotes lateral water movement and wets a greater volume of soil. Medium-textured soils usually perform well, but there can be problems with some fine-textured soils. By adding humus or compost to the soil, this problem can be solved.

Salts tend to concentrate at the soil surface and constitute a potential hazard because light rains can move them into the root zone, where they can burn roots. Therefore, when rain occurs after a period of salt accumulation, irrigation should continue on schedule until about 2 inches of rain has fallen, to ensure leaching of salts out of the root zone.

During drip irrigation, salts also concentrate below the surface of the soil wetted by each emitter. Drying of the soil between irrigations may cause a reverse movement of soil water, thus transferring salt from the perimeter back toward the emitter. Water movement must always be away from the emitter to avoid salt damage.

If circumstances cause an interruption of irrigation, plant damage can occur rather quickly because the ability of roots to forage for nutrients and water is limited to the small volume of soil wetted. Irrigation must be frequent, which means daily or on alternate days during the major growing season. The rate of water movement by capillary action decreases rapidly as the soil dries and becomes zero if the soil cracks. Finally, rodents often chew polyethylene lateral tubing. Rodent control, or use of polyvinylchloride (PVC) laterals, are possible solutions.

Although there may be some problems with drip system irrigation, there are solutions, as we shall see. And if properly installed, a drip system should be relatively trouble free. Let's turn to the various types to consider.

Drip Watering Systems

Drip irrigation is the frequent, slow application of water only to plant roots through emitters (holes) located at selected points along water-delivery lines. The lines are small-diameter plastic tubes installed on the surface of or below the soil. Some drip system manufacturers also offer misting and sprinkler emitters. The misting is concentrated in a small area round the plant, as is the sprinkling process. The difference between conventional sprinklers and misters is that in drip watering, the mister and sprinkler emitters deposit the water directly on the plant, not around it.

A basic drip system is a network of flexible plastic pipes and tubes of graduated sizes. A large pipe (generally ½ inch in diameter) brings the water to the site; a series of smaller main lines connects to the large pipe (usually ⅜ inch or ¼ inch in diameter). The lateral lines are placed parallel to the plants on or just below the surface of the ground. The water is discharged from the lateral lines through emitters.

The emitters allow a slow trickle of water to moisten the immediate root zone. In a grid system, pipes are usually placed above ground.

The main concern of the average gardener when using drip systems is being sure not to overload the setup—too many emitters in a given system (each manufacturer supplies information about this). If the lines have too many emitters, the regulated and steady flow of water is interrupted. The system will still work, but not efficiently.

The advent of the plastics industry made drip irriga-

Methods of watering

T-BRANCH SURFACE DRIP WATERING

CANVAS SOAKER HOSE

PLASTIC SOAKER HOSE

BUBBLER

tion possible on large and small scales. After World War II, plastic was developed that was flexible and chemically resistant. The earliest drip systems consisted of small-diameter (1-millimeter; mm) plastic capillary tubes connected to larger pipes. The systems were originally laid underground, but because clogging often occurred since no good filtration system had been devised, the pipes were eventually moved above ground. This innovation made it easy to keep the pipes free of debris and soil, and also put the water directly above the root system—in essence, where it was needed.

As discussed earlier, the water must be filtered so it does not clog the emitters. Most drip systems have a filter unit that removes particles that might clog the

A typical row layout showing the drip setup—ideal for flower beds or row crops. One turn of the faucet and water is in motion.   *Photo courtesy Sub Terrain Irrigation Co.*

Closeup showing watering pattern of row plan drip system. *Photo courtesy Sub Terrain Irrigation Co.*

workings of the hoses. Pressure regulators or valves to control the flow of water are also used. Systems can be manual or automatic. The equipment for drip irrigation comes in a variety of shapes, sizes, and costs (see Chapter 5).

Who installs a drip system? You can do it yourself, and I hope you will (after reading this book)—but you can also have someone else do it for you if you do not have the time or inclination to do the labor yourself. Almost any company offering sprinkler installation will also be able to install drip watering methods. Call and inquire.

You may want to have a landscape architect plan a system for your garden and have it installed. Consult professionals who are listed in the Yellow Pages of your telephone book. Always ask if the person is familiar with drip gardening and whether she or he has samples of work. And of course, first discuss and agree on a price. (See also Chapter 5.)

Where to Buy Drip Systems

Many hardware stores now carry the component parts for drip setups—you can buy pipe, emitters, and so forth. Kits with all parts for small and large areas are also available but usually cost more than if you put together your own system from components. During the drought years of 1976 and 1977, many manufacturers jumped on the bandwagon and quickly designed, manufactured, and pushed many types of drip irrigation kits. Most of these companies have since disappeared, but the suppliers who were in business for many years before the drought, and who pioneered the concept, are still doing a thriving business.

Another source for drip systems is the Yellow Pages of your phonebook, under "Sprinklers" or "Irrigation." There are also wholesale equipment manufacturers who will refer you to their dealers in your city. And of course, the suppliers listed in Chapter 5 will furnish brochures, another source of pertinent information to get you started on the better way to watering plants. Some of these manufacturers are known for their commercial irrigation equipment, but many carry home gardening systems as well.

On the next page: A typical drip installation for shrubs. The emitter is placed on the large pipe, and spur lines run directly to the root zone of the plant. Adquate water is continually available. *Photo by Michael Jay*

Kits

Kits with all parts included are also available from suppliers. The kits have been designed for small or large gardens, for patio plants, and so on—generally in three sizes to cover three areas.

Soaker hose system in which water trickles from plastic hose; some soaker systems are part of the drip concept if pressure is regulated. Other soakers are merely hoses with holes. *Photos by Michael Jay*

Soakers

In drip systems, emitters are the key; they distribute and regulate water slowly and steadily. Water is thus released at a specific flow rate. The most primitive drip system, known as the *soaker,* consists simply of a hose with holes in it. These systems are cheaper than standard drip systems, but they cannot do the same kind of job. Soakers generally get clogged, and they have no pressure-sensitive mechanisms to control water flow or rate of delivery of water for, say, a garden or a hill. True, soakers save water, and they do release it slowly, but they cannot compare with drip systems which yield bigger and better plants and save more water. However, soakers are still better than conventional hoses and sprinklers. The soaker hoses come in plastic or canvas; I have found the canvas ones to be better than the plastic hoses.

Ooze Systems and Bubbler Heads

In addition to the standard drip systems, there are other watering concepts whereby moisture is delivered slowly to plants. The ooze system consists of a series of perforated flexible pipes installed about 4 to 6 inches below the ground. Pipes are placed about 18 inches apart for row crops or ground covers, or they can be set adjacent to shrubs or trees. The principle here is that no water flows on the surface, so runoff and evaporation are almost eliminated. The commercial soaker hose is similar, except that it is used above the ground.

Another variation is the bubbler head, a metal can-shaped container with holes that can be attached to a regular garden hose. Bubbler heads are arranged in the same manner as sprinklers; they are placed one for each shrub or tree set directly into a planter box. Bubbler heads flow at about 1 gallon per minute (gpm), and the water does not spray, so it feeds directly into the plant. Water soaks in deeply, and there is less evaporation than with conventional spray heads.

Homemade Drip Systems

You can make your own drip system by punching small holes with a nail or an ice pick in the bottom of a coffee can or plastic container. Then place each container near the base of a plant that needs watering. Fill the can with water and let the water from the can drip into the soil. Primitive, assuredly—but the principle is there.

There are several ways to utilize hoses and convert them into a type of drip watering setup. If you have an old hose with a leak in it, make an inexpensive drip hose out of it by notching the hose with a knife at various points. The larger the hole, the more water will escape. Lay the hose on the surface of the soil near row plants for an inexpensive quasi-drip system of watering, or place hoses around trees or shrubs for moisture.

The same type of watering system can be used for planter boxes (as shown in our drawings), or hoses with holes can be stationed at the top of fences to furnish water to plants below.

For example, step-down planter box irrigation is an

Step-down planter box irrigation

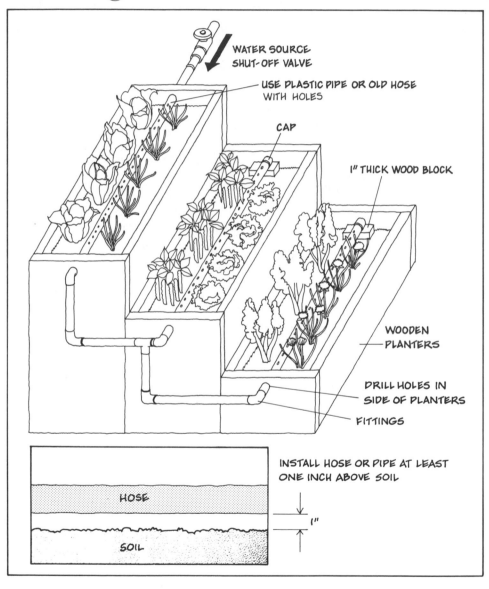

WATER SOURCE
SHUT-OFF VALVE

USE PLASTIC PIPE OR OLD HOSE
WITH HOLES

CAP

1" THICK WOOD BLOCK

WOODEN
PLANTERS

DRILL HOLES IN
SIDE OF PLANTERS

FITTINGS

INSTALL HOSE OR PIPE AT LEAST
ONE INCH ABOVE SOIL

HOSE

1"

SOIL

Homemade drip system concepts

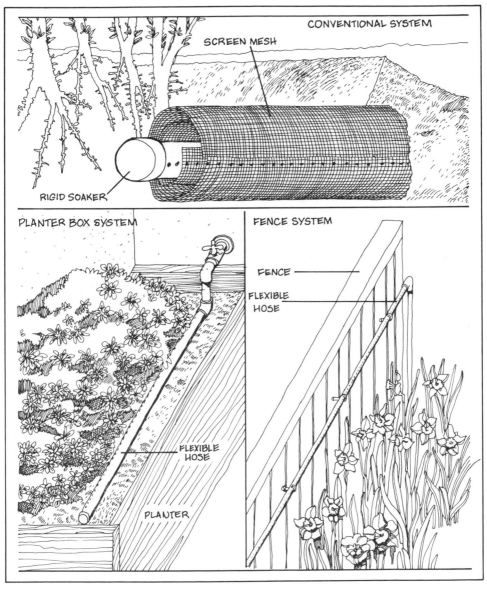

CONVENTIONAL SYSTEM

SCREEN MESH

RIGID SOAKER

PLANTER BOX SYSTEM

FENCE SYSTEM

FENCE

FLEXIBLE HOSE

FLEXIBLE HOSE

PLANTER

Hose on box

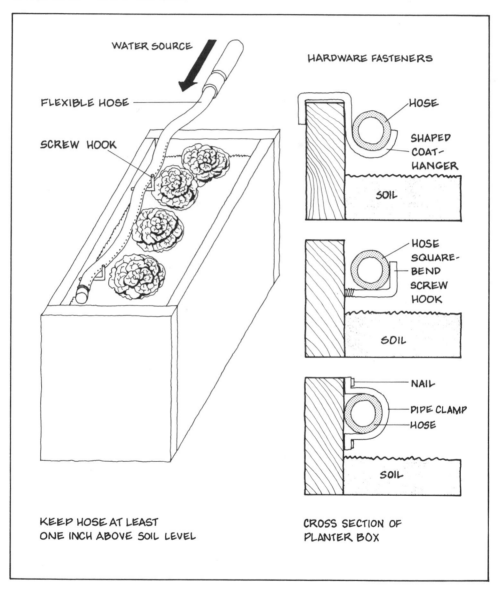

WATER SOURCE

HARDWARE FASTENERS

FLEXIBLE HOSE

HOSE

SCREW HOOK

SHAPED COAT-HANGER

SOIL

HOSE
SQUARE-BEND SCREW HOOK

SOIL

NAIL

PIPE CLAMP

HOSE

SOIL

KEEP HOSE AT LEAST
ONE INCH ABOVE SOIL LEVEL

CROSS SECTION OF
PLANTER BOX

efficient and simple way to provide drip watering to a contained planter box garden. Plants thrive and you do not need to stand endlessly watering with a hose.

Drill holes throughout the sides of the planter boxes to match the diameter of fittings (at plumbing or hardware suppliers). Use hose couplings to attach plastic pipe or old hosing. Make holes in the pipe or hose with a nail or an ice pick. When the setup is complete, water runs through the pipes in the top box to the second box and then to the lower planter so that with one turn of the faucet you can water three planters. Remember to insert hose caps at the ends of the two hoses in the bottom boxes. Position the hoses so they are about 1 inch above the soil. Flexible hose will have a tendency to sag but this will not affect the operation of the drip watering. The hoses should not exceed 48 inches in length.

A variation on the same theme is to attach hoses with wire or coat hangars, as shown in the drawing.

You can make an underground drip system by wrapping a pipe or plastic hose in hardware cloth as shown in the drawing. This is an inexpensive way to water trees and shrubs, and installation takes only a few hours.

4. Selecting a Drip System for Your Garden

FROM THE drawings and diagrams in this book you can see that there are many drip or soaker watering systems for your property. Which system should you choose? Should the pipe be above ground or below it? How should you lay it out—with spur line, in a channel pattern, or what? The answers to these questions depend on the type of your garden and the topography of your land. But in almost every case there is a drip system to help you water your plants properly. Spacing is the key word—how you select the necessary emitters and lay out the hoses can come later.

Planning the System

The only safe way to plan the drip system is first to sketch it on paper. You do not need to be an artist or a landscape architect; on a sheet of graph paper (sold at art stores), measure off the garden area in feet and inches. Now draw in the existing plants; use a different shape for shrubs, trees, flowers. It is not necessary to know the landscape architectural symbols—just draw shapes for each plant so you have a plan or aerial-type drawing.

Will it be possible to drip water to all areas of the garden? This depends on the size of the plot. Generally, the average garden of say 20 × 40 feet can certainly have a total drip watering setup. Initially you can install a small system and then add on to it later.

You can drip water to almost any plant, even grasses, although in the case of lawns the soaker drip system is used rather than the conventional drip system with emitters. Seed gardens can be watered with soakers as well.

In many cases you will need several drip setups for an entire garden area. Map out the site with existing plants as already suggested, and then sketch in systems as they would apply—a row pattern in one area perhaps (vegetables and flowers), or a point or grid pattern in another place. The selection of the system depends on how many plants are in the garden and the distance between them.

Now study the drawings carefully and then decide where to lay hoses and install emitters. Follow that plan! The shortest distance between two points is still a straight line—use that as a guide. You can easily pattern your garden with a drip system from a simple sketch.

On the Ground?
Above the Ground?

It is difficult to determine just what method of application is best: above- or below-ground installation. Most gardens have above-ground setups, but experts argue that below ground is where pipes should be. The answer lies in your own garden—if hoses and pipes on soil are conspicuous, then the more expensive underground system might be the solution. In many gardens, the

Vegetable garden soaker system

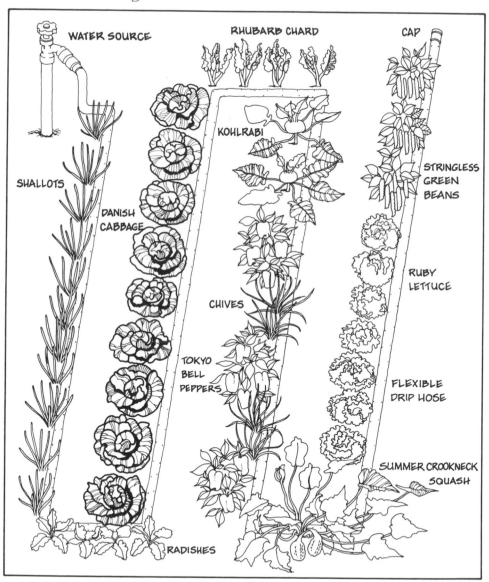

WATER SOURCE

RHUBARB CHARD

CAP

SHALLOTS

DANISH CABBAGE

KOHLRABI

STRINGLESS GREEN BEANS

RUBY LETTUCE

CHIVES

TOKYO BELL PEPPERS

FLEXIBLE DRIP HOSE

SUMMER CROOKNECK SQUASH

RADISHES

placement of hoses on the soil does not seem to detract from the overall appearance because plants will cover the hoses as they grow.

On-the-ground system using a sprinkler mister to provide steady moisture to plant roots. *Photo courtesy Drip and Mist Watering Co.*

How Much or How Often to Water?

Drip watering solves the dilemma of how much to water because it is possible by using certain equations to gauge the amount of water needed to replenish that evaporated from the soil and transpired through the leaves of the plants. In these equations the amount of water required by various plants depends on the kind of soil

On-the-ground hillside drip system; water flows directly to the plant roots, steadily and slowly, with minimum runoff. *Photo courtesy Sub Terrain Irrigation Co.*

and the effects of vapor pressure of wind and temperatures. However, you really need not concern yourself with these equations.

The wet zone (the area around the roots of the plant) is what is vital. You have to consider the size and shape of the wet zone, which will vary according to (1) the type of soil, (2) the rate at which the plant takes moisture from the soil in relation to the number of emitters used, and (3) the rate at which the emitters discharge water. Water moves downward by gravity and spreads in all directions by capillary action. In fine soil, capillary forces are stronger than the gravitational ones, so the wet zone is circular in appearance, whereas in coarse soil, which does not retain water for any length of time, the wet zone is elliptical in size.

Water should be applied slowly so it will be absorbed and not run off from application points. Runoff and ponding can be avoided by stopping the water and then turning it on again later. The time interval between one application of water and the next may range from 1 to 16 hours. If the time is more than 16 hours, you would have to increase the number of emitters.

To aid you in determining how much water certain groups of plants need—trees, shrubs, flowers— manufacturers generally include in their literature various watering charts (some of these are in Chapter 5). The charts are meant only as guidelines; watering needs will depend on plant type, sun and wind exposure, and soil composition. Climatic conditions vary throughout the United States; for example, in desert areas plants may require many more moisture applications than are described in suppliers' charts. Your own experience with your garden will dictate changes in frequency, volume, and watering times.

Below-ground drip installation showing emitter at base of plant.   *Photo courtesy Drip and Mist Watering Co.*

In this photo the dark area indicates that moisture from drip system watering has reached plant roots.   *Photo courtesy Drip and Mist Watering Co.*

Row Irrigation

Row irrigation is exactly what it says: the drip system lines (tubing) are laid next to plants in rows; this setup is suitable for plants such as flowers, vegetables, and herbs grown in rows. One company offers a row system consisting of 15 feet of mainline hose and 100 feet of emitter hose and connections. The kit covers an area of approximately 150 square feet, or 15 × 10 feet. The cost is modest (about $20), and the setup requires only a few hours to install.

The row system of drip watering helps to cut down on weeds because moisture is applied only to the plants you want to grow; it is difficult for weeds to sprout where there is no water.

Point Irrigation

Another system of drip watering is point (grid) irrigation, in which spur lines are connected to a mainline hose for watering specific bushes, flowers, and vegetables spaced well apart. One company offers a kit for about $20 containing 10 feet of mainline hose, twelve emitters on 48-inch tubes, and connections suitable for an area of, say, 100 square feet, or 10 × 10 feet.

The installation of the drip system for your garden—the actual laying of the pipes—is the difficult

Typical row installation using drip system; note emitters placed strategically at plant base. *Photo courtesy Sub Terrain Irrigation Co.*

part. Once the system has been mapped and laid out there is little work for you other than turning on the water. And for each garden, different types of systems for layouts are necessary.

Flower garden irrigation

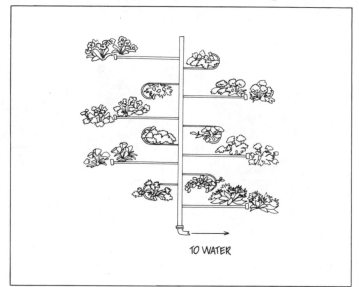

TO WATER

House plant irrigation

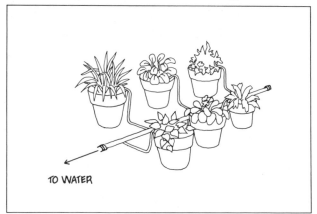

TO WATER

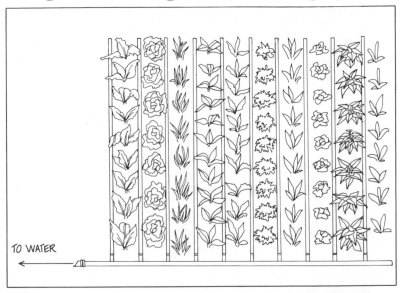

Vegetable garden irrigation

TO WATER

The Garden

Let us start with a general garden plan—that is, flower borders and beds, with ornamental shrubs and trees as the background. The center of the garden or part of it is either a lawn or patio. In this type of garden we opt for a perimeter system of hose, with spur lines and emitters coming off the main hose line, which is standard ¼-inch hose. For a 20- by 30-foot garden the cost is no more than $40. Because most of the plants are tall, the line is set on top of the ground, with emitters at specific places: about twelve emitters near specific plants.

In a cutting garden we use a U-shaped layout for the drip system. Here the hoses are laid out in a conventional U, parallel to the rows of plants; this, by the

Terrace garden irrigation

Flower garden irrigation

way, is an easy system to lay out and works very well.

For the vegetable garden a U pattern again could be used, or a grid pattern of piping works well. Vegetables require a lot of water, so the spacing of the emitters is closer than in, say, an ornamental garden.

Vegetable / Fruit Gardens

A drip watering system for a vegetable garden is a blessing. Not only will it save you time, but it will save you weeding and the fuming and fussing involved in vegetable growing. Be sure you have good soil—rich and porous—and the drip system will do the rest.

Although the cost of the drip system for your vegetable garden may well be more than the cost of hoses or sprinklers—or just about the same—the amount of the resulting produce will be far greater than with conventional watering. You will have bushels of vegetables, larger and sweeter than if you raised the crops by conventional watering methods. The proof is well established in technical bulletins available from various manufacturers.

If you are growing fruit trees, the drip system is a must—it will produce larger yields with very little work. Conventional watering systems for fruit trees leave a lot to be desired, and I think everyone, if at all possible, should have fruit trees because the pure fresh fruit, with its wonderful flavor, picked from your own trees is a satisfaction indeed. Remember that the fruit you buy in stores is at least one week, if not two weeks old. In such a situation much of the goodness and vitamins are long gone, so be healthy and wise and grow your own fruit.

Flower Gardens

If you must watch your gardening budget, the flower garden is the one place where you can install a small drip system and let nature (rain) do the rest. Even two drip kits will supply moisture for the average flower garden; total cost will be about $40. Drip watering eliminates most weeds, so the money spent is well worth it.

Hillside Gardens

If you have ever gardened on a hillside, you know how difficult it is to get water to your plants because it runs off. The water is being applied so quickly that little of it reaches and is maintained by the plants. Drip systems solve this problem because they feed water slowly to plants, thus reducing runoff. For successful watering of a hillside area, the system can be laid out in parallel rows spaced every 24 inches. Pressure-sensitive emitters should be used on hillsides so water is distributed evenly to all plants.

Trees and Shrubs

It may at first seem like a lot of work, and somewhat foolish as well, to install emitters close to shrubs and trees that are widely separated. Yet trees and shrubs are expensive plants, so the nominal cost of an initial drip system installation can assure beautiful greenery for years. Once again, the initial layout is what is important. The point system is good for trees and shrubs, which, by necessity because of their size, have to be placed far apart.

Lawns

Even a small lawn can add a note of elegance to a garden, but gardeners often forgo lawns because of the watering and upkeep—they require too much care and watering. However, that beautiful carpet of green can be achieved with little effort if you use subsurface drip soaker systems. These systems dispense with sprinkler heads that are likely to clog or spray you, and you can even walk on the lawn while it is being watered.

Soaker underground watering saves both water and

This dry hillside presented a major watering problem for the homeowner, but it was easily solved with a drip watering system. *Photo courtesy Sub Terrain Irrigation Co.*

Typical drip installation for a tree; the emitter is at rear and pipes are underground.
Photo courtesy Drip and Mist Watering Co.

time. Two kinds of tubing are usually used in these systems. One, a black plastic tubing, is actually a tube within a tube—water is dispensed through holes in the tube at 4- to 12-inch intervals; 8-mil thickness is used. Another type of tubing is flexible PVC (polyvinylchloride).

Both kinds of tubing are installed by digging trenches and laying tube, and then backfilling and seeding or plugging the trench marks. If possible, the system should be installed before planting a new lawn. Water for these systems requires an in-line filtering unit to prevent clogging, and both systems operate at below-normal water pressure. For dual wall tubing, use a 15-psi pressure regulator or inexpensive flow-control fittings. For porous PVC tubing, use a flow-control valve. (Drip system suppliers sell these hardware items.)

After installing the system and seeding a new lawn, hand-water daily until the grass is about 2 to 4 inches high. Then change to underground watering. The system works by capillary motion—water is drawn from wet areas to dry spaces between tubes. The lawn should be watered about every other day, for about 1 hour. However, this varies according to the condition of your soil and your climate.

Here are the instructions for installing a lawn watering system:

1) Check with your local water authorities to determine if an antisiphon device is necessary at the main water control.

2) Install the screen filter.

3) Divide the area to be watered into 500-square-foot sections.

4) Make a continuous loop around the lawn area

with ½-inch poly tubing. Use 12-inch spacing. Lay tubing with holes up, and connect each end to the ½-inch
tubing.

5) Install a T so you can run the clean tube to a convenient area, and leave the cap exposed for easy access.*

Container Gardens

A drip system for a box or container garden requires a
somewhat different installation because the lines must
be run in the planter boxes. For my deck garden, which
is a box arrangement, the hose is secured to a wooden
fence approximately 4 inches above the soil line of the
wooden boxes. The slow trickle of water supplied con-
tinuously to the plants makes them grow rapidly. Before
I installed the drip system, the soil was forever drying
out because soil in boxes dries out much faster than soil
in the ground. Ground plants can always reach out for
moisture; roots confined to boxes cannot.

My planter boxes are approximately 4 to 6 feet long,
so installation was not difficult; however, if you have
single boxes, there is a problem. You can still run a single emitter somewhere overhead if there is a suitable
wooden post or other wood member to which the hose
or pipe can be attached. If there is not, then you must
water by conventional means.

* By permission of Drip and Mist Watering Systems of San Juan
Capistrano, California.

This contained garden at an entrance is drip watered; hardware is hidden; pipes are underground. *Photo courtesy Drip and Mist Watering Co.*

General List of Plants

The following list of trees, shrubs, and perennials is to help you determine which plants need a lot of water (wet soil conditions) and which require little water (dry soil conditions).

For Wet Soil Conditions

TREES, DECIDUOUS

Acer rubrum
(red maple)
Alnus glutinosa
(black alder)
Betula populifolia
(gray birch)
Gleditsia aquatica
(water locust)
Liquidambar styraciflua
(sweet gum)
Platanus occidentalis
(buttonwood)
Quercus palustris
(pin oak)
Salix alba
(white willow)
Tilia americana
(American linden)

TREES, EVERGREEN

Abies balsamea
(balsam fir)
Thuja occidentalis
(arborvitae)
Tsuga canadensis
(hemlock)

SHRUBS

Alnus (various)
(alders)

Amelanchier canadensis
(shadblow service berry)
Andromeda species
(andromeda)
Aronia arbutifolia
(red chokeberry)
Calluna vulgaris
(heather)
Clethra alnifolia
(summer sweet)
Cornus alba
(tatarian dogwood)
Cornus stolonifera
(red osier)
Cornus sanguinea
(bloodtwig dogwood)
Hypericum densiflorum
(dense hypericum)
Ilex glabra
(inkberry)
Ilex verticillata
(winterberry)
Kalmia angustifolia
(sheep laurel)
Ligustrum amurense
(amur privet)
Pieris floribunda
(mountain andromeda)
Rhododendron
(rhododendron)
Sabal minor
(dwarf palmetto)

Salix (various)
  (willow)
Spiraea menziesii
  (spirea)
Spiraea tomentosa
Vaccinum corymbosum
  (highbush blueberry)
Viburnum alnifolium
  (hobblebush)
Viburnum cassinoides
  (withe rod)
Viburnum dentatum
  (arrowwood)
Viburnum lentago
  (nannyberry)
Viburnum sieboldii
  (siebold viburnum)

PERENNIALS

Arundo "Donax"
  (giant reed)
Asclepias incarnata
  (swamp milkweed)
Caltha palustris
  (marsh marigold)
Equisetum hyemale
  (horsetail)

Gentiana asclepiadea
  (willow gentian)
Helenium (various)
  (Helen's flower)
Hibiscus moscheutos
  (swamp rose mallow)
Iris pseudacorus
  (yellow flag)
Iris versicolor
  (blue flag)
Lobelia cardinalis
  (cardinal flower)
Lythrum (various)
  (loosestrife)
Monarda didyma
  (bee balm)
Myosotis scorpiodes
  (true forget-me-not)
Oenothera (various)
  (evening primrose)
Sarracenia purpurea
  (pitcher plants)
Saxifraga
  (saxifrage)
Vinca
  (periwinkle)

For Dry Soil Conditions

TREES, DECIDUOUS

Acer ginnala
  (Amur maple)
Acer tataricum
  (tatarian maple)
Alanthus altissima
  (tree of heaven)
Betula pendula
  (European birch)
Betula populifolia
  (gray birch)
Carya glabra
  (pignut)

Cotinus coggygria
  (smoke tree)
Populus alba
  (white poplar)
Populus tremuloides
  (quaking aspen)
Prunus cerasus
  (sour cherry)
Prunus serotina
  (black cherry)
Quercus ruber
  (cork oak)
Robinia pseudoacacia
  (black locust)

Trees, Evergreen

Juniperus chinensis
(Chinese juniper)
Juniperus virginiana
(eastern red cedar)
Picea alba
(Canadian spruce)
Picea abies (*excelsa*)
(Norway spruce)
Pinus mugo
(Swiss mountain pine)
Pinus rigida
(pitch pine)
Pinus strobus
(white pine)
Pinus sylvestris
(Scots pine)

Shrubs

Arbutus unedo
(strawberry tree)
Arctostaphylos uva-ursi
(bearberry)
Berberis, several
(barberry)
Betula glandulosa
Betula nana
Buddleia alternifolia
(fountain buddleia)
Ceanothus americanus
(New Jersey tea)
Cotoneaster
(contoneaster)
Cytisus
(broom)
Elaeagnus angustifolia
(Russian olive)
Euonymus japonica
(evergreen euonymus)
Genistra tinctoria
(dyer's greenweed)

Hamamelis virginiana
(common witch hazel)
Hypericum spathulatum
(shrubby Saint-Johns-
wort)
Juniperus communis
(juniper)
Juniperus horizontalis
(creeping juniper)
Kolkwitzia amabilis
(beauty bush)
Ligustrum vulgare
(common privet)
Nerium oleander
(oleander)
Pittosporum tobira
(Japanese pittosporum)
Potentilla fruticosa
(cinquefoil)
Prunus besseyi
(western sand cherry)
Prunus maritima
(beach plum)
Pyracantha coccinea
(scarlet firethron)
Raphiolepis umbellata
(hawthorn)
Rhamnus alaternus
Rhamnus frangula
(alder buckthorn)
Rhus (various)
(sumac)
Robinia hispida
(rose acacia)
Robinia pseudoacacia
(locust)
Robinia viscosa
(clammy locust)
Rosa (various)
(rose)
Salix species
(willow)

Tamarix species
(tamarix)
Viburnum lantana
(wayfaring tree)
Viburnum lentago
(nannyberry)

PERENNIALS

Achillea (various)
(yarrow)
Ajuga reptans
(carpet bugle)
Anthemis tinctoria
(golden marguerite)
Artemisia pycnocephala
Asclepias tuberosa
(butterfly weed)
Aster novae-angliae
(New England aster)
Callirhoe involucrata
(poppy mallow)
Cerastium tomentosum
(snow-in-summer)
Coreopsis grandiflora
(tickseed)

Dianthus (various)
(pinks)
Echinops exaltatus
(globe thistle)
Echium
Gazania hybrids
Geranium grandiflorum
(cranesbill)
Gypsophila paniculata
(baby's breath)
Helianthus (various)
(sunflower)
Limonium latifolium
(statice, sea lavender)
Papaver nudicaule
(Iceland poppy)
Phlox subulata
(moss pink)
Potentilla atrosanguinea
(cinquefoil)
Rudbeckia hirta
(coneflower)
Veronica (various)
(speedwell)
Yucca filamentosa
(Adam's needle)

5. Drip Irrigation Equipment and Manufacturers

IN THIS CHAPTER we will deal with the more technical aspects of drip irrigation: the actual equipment. Generally you will need to know the number of emitters necessary, tubing needs, types of valves, what controllers to use, types of screens and filters your system should have, and so on. Equipment basically consists of tubing (in several diameters), lateral lines, emitters, main lines, and filter attachments.

The main feature of a drip system is its monitoring device—an emitter—that is placed near the plant to be irrigated. Some emitters are small mechanisms plugged directly into rigid or flexible piping; others are ⅛-inch tubing inserted into adaptors on the main lines. The emitter allows a very low rate of water (usually 1 to 2 gallons per hour—(gph) to pass through it to the plant.

Each manufacturer has its own hardware and component parts, so there are different installations for each system. Here we look at several systems and given general directions for each one. Prices are competitive, and it is difficult to say which system is best. (All have been

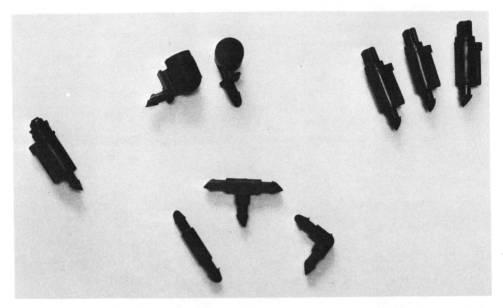

The top row shows various emitters (1-gallon, 2-gallon, and so forth). These emitters punch into main lines without sealant. At the bottom of the photo, various connectors for piping are visible. *Photo courtesy Drip and Mist Watering Co.*

tested and work well.) Citing certain manufacturers as examples should not be considered an endorsement for any one system.

Emitters (Sub Terrain Irrigation Co.)

There are more than fifty different emitters on the market. Emitters control the water flow from the lateral lines of the main hose into the soil by decreasing the pressure from the inside to the outside of the lateral, thus allowing the water to emerge as drops through small holes, larger holes in series, long passageways, vortex chambers, discs, steel balls, and so on. There are four types of emitters as manufactured by the Sub Terrain Irrigation Company: (1) fancy, protected holes in the line; (2) pressure loss; (3) pressure compensating; and (4) automatic moisture sensing. Type 1 usually provides some guard to discourage bugs from clogging the line. These emit-

A typical 2-gallon emitter (magnified), and at the right, its component parts. *Photos by Michael Jay*

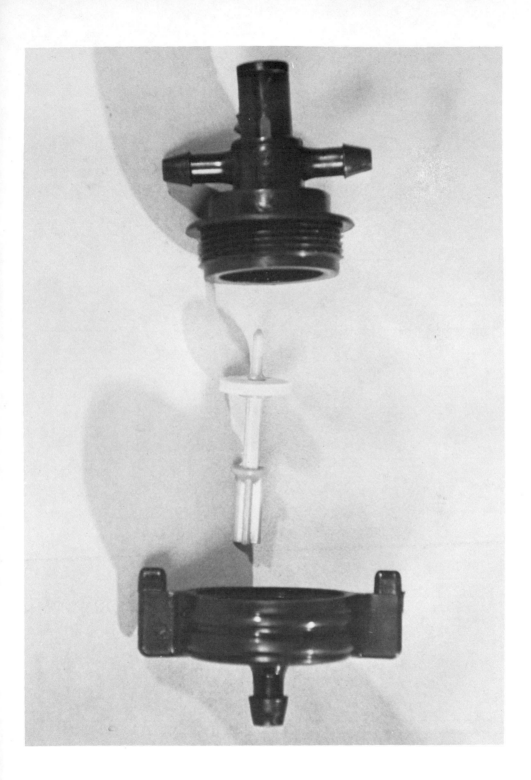

Types of drip systems

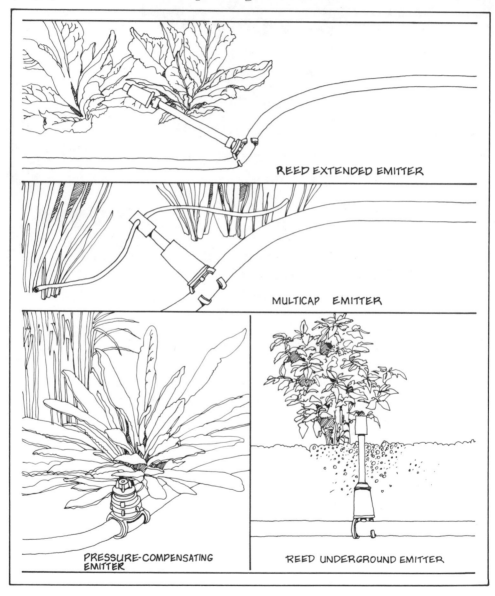

REED EXTENDED EMITTER

MULTICAP EMITTER

PRESSURE-COMPENSATING EMITTER

REED UNDERGROUND EMITTER

Drip emitters

REED IN-LINE EMITTER

REED SNAP-ON EMITTER

DRIP-EZE TAKE-APART

Underground emitters

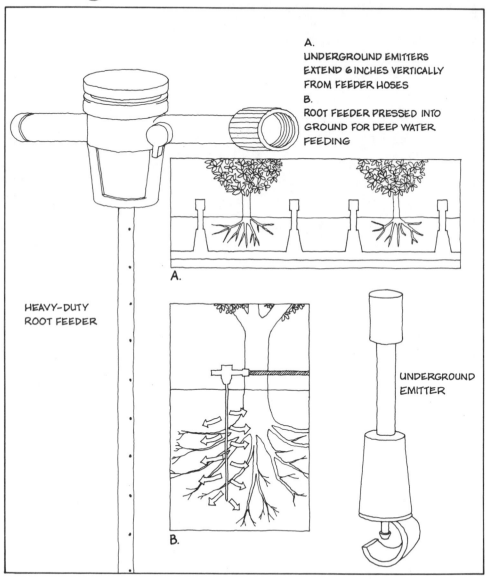

A.
UNDERGROUND EMITTERS
EXTEND 6 INCHES VERTICALLY
FROM FEEDER HOSES
B.
ROOT FEEDER PRESSED INTO
GROUND FOR DEEP WATER
FEEDING

A.

HEAVY-DUTY
ROOT FEEDER

B.

UNDERGROUND
EMITTER

Types of emitters

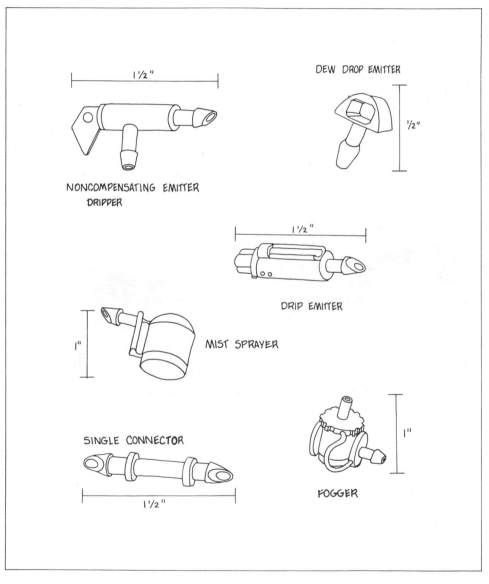

1 1/2"

DEW DROP EMITTER

1/2"

NONCOMPENSATING EMITTER
DRIPPER

1 1/2"

DRIP EMITTER

1"

MIST SPRAYER

SINGLE CONNECTOR

1"

1 1/2"

FOGGER

ters require careful attention to tube size, restrictors, and flow-control valves to make them emit equal amounts of water for the full length of the run. Type 2, the pressure-loss emitter, directs water through a maze that causes the water to lose its pressure and emerge as drops. Types 1 and 2 are more subject to clogging because of their fixed-orifice size and their inability to flush automatically. Elevation and pressure variances within the lines cause different flow rates. Although generally lower in initial price than emitter types 3 and 4, types 1 and 2 can be expensive to maintain.

The Drip-Eze Manufacturing Co. emitter has clamp-ons; again the emitter is inserted into the main pipe, and also clamps in place, as shown at the right.   *Photos by Michael Jay*

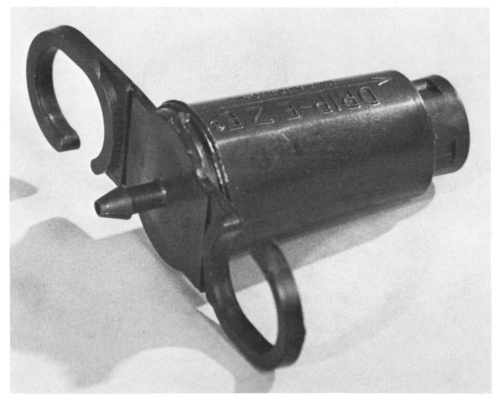

Type 3 (pressure-compensating) emitters, like Sub Terrain's Standard (ST), Flapper (STF), or Turbo-Flo (TF), act like tiny valves. They emit constant drips of water whose pressures vary little between 15 and 45 psi because they retain low, even pressure (compensate) for the entire length of the tubing even while dripping. The emitter closest to the water source has approximately the same flow rate as one 500 feet down the line. Water automatically flushes through a variable-size orifice every time the system is turned on or off; the emitter can be flushed manually at any time, and it can be taken apart and cleaned. The Standard emitter can be buried because dirt will not siphon back into the line.

Sub Terrain's Flapper emitter has the largest size variable orifice. This emitter is recommended for dirtier water and for water from wells and lakes. It automatically flushes during on and off cycles, and can be buried only if spaghetti tubing is added to transport the water above the surface. The Standard Sub Terrain emitter is usually recommended for landscape work, whereas the Flapper is extensively used in agriculture.

The Turbo-Flo emitter compensates for pressure changes automatically and flushes manually. Like the Flapper and Standard, it accurately emits the precise number of gallons per hour year after year.

Emitters should be checked visually each week for correct flow. As their performance builds confidence, the intervals between checking may be increased. Take precise measurements at least twice a year by catching the flow from a number of emitters in a calibrated cylinder for exactly 1 minute. Emitter performance problems or incorrect pressure control in lateral lines are revealed by such measurements.

Let's look at a typical emitter. The heart of an emit-

Component parts
of drip system

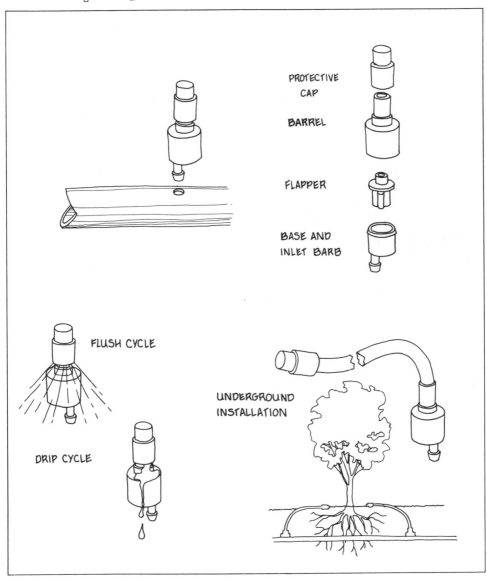

PROTECTIVE
CAP

BARREL

FLAPPER

BASE AND
INLET BARB

FLUSH CYCLE

UNDERGROUND
INSTALLATION

DRIP CYCLE

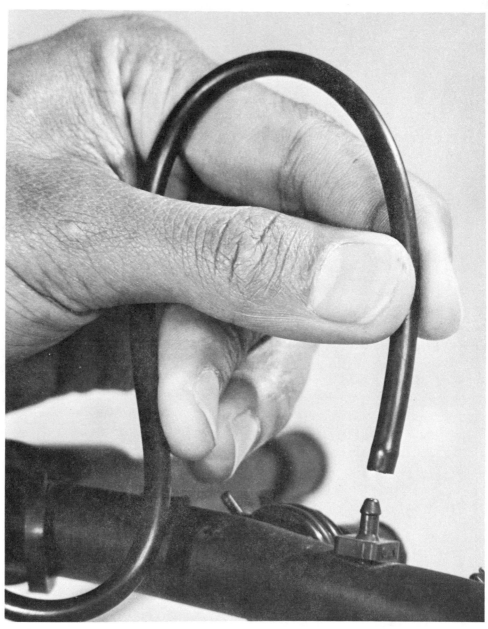

Installing spur line on main line; note special punch-in plug. *Photo by Michael Jay*

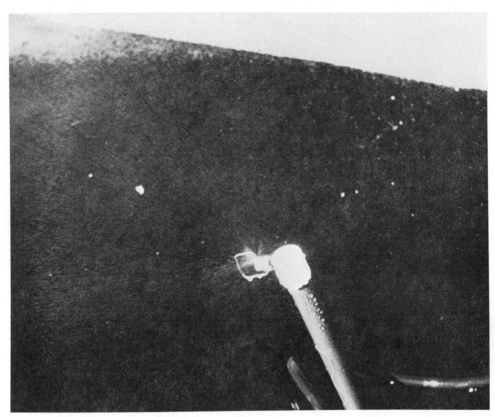

Special mister emitter for constant low-volume watering.   *Photo courtesy Sub Terrain Irrigation Co.*

ter is a silicone diaphragm. This simple one-piece component is open and flushes through a large 1.100-mm orifice under start-up pressure. It automatically closes to drip mode at 1 psi. A short ¼-inch flow path evenly regulates flow over a wide pressure range of from 10 to 50 psi. While water is flowing, the diaphragm vibrates to keep the drip slot free of dirt buildup. The diaphragm again flushes when the system is turned off, or it can be flushed manually.

Installing Emitters   At least five-eighths of the root zone of each plant must be covered by the water-penetration pattern of the emitters. Run flexible poly tubing within the drip line of each plant or tree. Loop trees that are 10 feet or taller with tubing connected to evenly spaced emitters. Emitters must be equidistant for trees of this height in order to assure even watering of the complete root system. You can insert ⅛-inch spaghetti tubing into the ½- or ¾-inch poly lines for laterals not exceeding 10 feet; then push the emitter into the end of the small tubing. Use a hole punch with a 0.100-mm bit for Standard (ST) or Turbo-Flo (TF) emitters, a 0.115-mm bit for a Flapper (STF) emitter, and a 0.135-mm bit for ⅛-inch spaghetti tubing. Hole punches are available from suppliers.

Lateral Lines

Emitters are connected to or are a part of the lateral (branch) lines, which usually are made of plastic and are of small diameter (⅜ to ¼ inch). These lines may cover long distances because the flows through them are of low pressure. Lateral lines are generally placed one per tree row or one per crop row or pair of rows, and should be installed as near level as possible, particularly for systems using pressures of less than 10 psi.

Water pressure in the laterals at the emitter connection affects the output of most emitters. A few types of laterals are pressure compensating within limits to maintain a constant outflow. Pressure control in the distribution system is generally necessary, and is accomplished by placing laterals as nearly as possible on the contour and by including an adjustment valve at the connection of each lateral to the main head on sloping ground. The

Typical installation of drip system

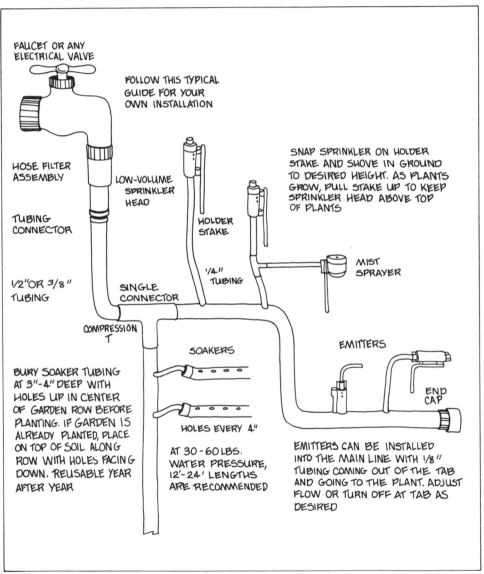

FAUCET OR ANY ELECTRICAL VALVE

FOLLOW THIS TYPICAL GUIDE FOR YOUR OWN INSTALLATION

HOSE FILTER ASSEMBLY

LOW-VOLUME SPRINKLER HEAD

SNAP SPRINKLER ON HOLDER STAKE AND SHOVE IN GROUND TO DESIRED HEIGHT. AS PLANTS GROW, PULL STAKE UP TO KEEP SPRINKLER HEAD ABOVE TOP OF PLANTS

TUBING CONNECTOR

HOLDER STAKE

1/2" OR 3/8" TUBING

SINGLE CONNECTOR

1/4" TUBING

MIST SPRAYER

COMPRESSION T

SOAKERS

EMITTERS

BURY SOAKER TUBING AT 3"-4" DEEP WITH HOLES UP IN CENTER OF GARDEN ROW BEFORE PLANTING. IF GARDEN IS ALREADY PLANTED, PLACE ON TOP OF SOIL ALONG ROW WITH HOLES FACING DOWN, REUSABLE YEAR AFTER YEAR

HOLES EVERY 4"

AT 30 - 60 LBS. WATER PRESSURE, 12'-24' LENGTHS ARE RECOMMENDED

END CAP

EMITTERS CAN BE INSTALLED INTO THE MAIN LINE WITH 1/8" TUBING COMING OUT OF THE TAB AND GOING TO THE PLANT. ADJUST FLOW OR TURN OFF AT TAB AS DESIRED

Mini system
drip irrigation

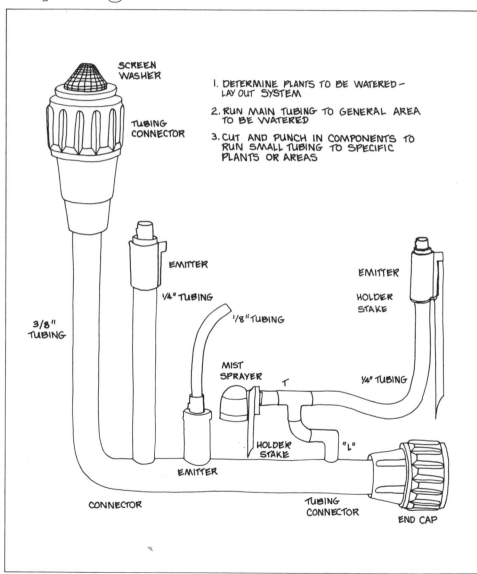

SCREEN
WASHER

TUBING
CONNECTOR

1. DETERMINE PLANTS TO BE WATERED — LAY OUT SYSTEM

2. RUN MAIN TUBING TO GENERAL AREA TO BE WATERED

3. CUT AND PUNCH IN COMPONENTS TO RUN SMALL TUBING TO SPECIFIC PLANTS OR AREAS

EMITTER

¼" TUBING

EMITTER

HOLDER
STAKE

⅛" TUBING

3/8"
TUBING

MIST
SPRAYER

T

¼" TUBING

HOLDER
STAKE

"L"

EMITTER

CONNECTOR

TUBING
CONNECTOR

END CAP

pressure at these adjustment valves should be checked periodically and the valves readjusted as needed.

Tubing

Drip systems have very low water quantity and pressure requirements, thus permitting the use of lower priced tubing. Tubing made of polyethylene and polybutylene offers three main advantages: (1) emitters can snap into it, saving the cost of Ts and risers, (2) its flexibility allows 30-inch-radius turns, and (3) no special tools or solvent welding cement are required. However, for drip use, only virgin, specially formulated tubing of ½ inch (0.580 inside diameter by 0.704 outside diameter) is recommended.

Compression Fittings

Agricultural Products, Inc., pioneered the development of compression fittings specifically for drip use. Originally, insert or barbed fittings with clamps were used, which created a problem. Water flows so slowly in drip tubing that during the day, because of the sun, water temperatures can reach 180°F when the tubing is exposed on the surface. At night, temperatures can drop to freezing. These temperature extremes cause expansion and contraction of the hoses; the barbs on insert fittings quickly stress the tubing, causing crazing or hairline cracks and then blowouts. The compression fittings developed by Agricultural Products do not insert; they surround the tubing. The greater the pressure (up to 60 psi), the better the fittings hold the joint. A simple wrist action "walks" the fitting onto the supply tubing, so no tools are required.

The chart of emitters and watering times in Table 3 is intended only as a guide; the type of soil and rate of penetration may dictate more or less watering time. As plants grow and require more water, it will probably be necessary to lengthen the watering period, add more emitters, or replace present emitters with larger capacity emitters. Watering time is based on Sub Terrain emit-

TABLE 3/EMITTER SELECTION CHART—WATERING GUIDE

Type of plant	No. of emitters	Rate (gph)	Special instructions	Watering time every other day (minutes)		
				Hot and windy	Warm	Cool
Hanging; potted; small shrubs	1	1	Use ⅛-inch tube to plant as lateral from ½-inch tube with emitter in end	30	20	10
Large shrubs	2 or 1	1 2	Snap-in emitters within drip line	30	20	10
10-foot trees	6 or 3	1 2	Snap-in emitters within drip line	30	20	10
20-foot trees	20 or 5	1 4	Snap-in emitters within drip line	30	20	10
Ground covers, flowers, vegetable gardens	1	1	Use one emitter every 2 feet, with tubing rows about 2 feet apart	240 (4 hr)	180 (3 hr)	120 (2 hr)

ters; there are 1-, 2-, and 4-gph emitters available. Water should be applied no more quickly than the soil will absorb it.

Filters and Screens

Generally, water used for drip irrigation must be cleaner than drinking water. Thus it must be kept free of sediment, soil, and mineral deposits. To accomplish this, various types of sand filters, cartridge filters, and screens of 100 to 200 mesh are used individually or in combination. The sand filter usually has manual or automatic backflushing devices for cleaning. The cartridge filter is changed when dirty, and screens are usually cleaned manually.

A filter can be a simple hose washer screen inserted into a garden hose swivel (available in hardware stores). For areas up to an acre, or where the water supply is nonpotable, use the larger cartridge-type hose washers, which have disposable filters or permanent stainless-steel screens. Larger installations on a potable water supply require filters from ¾ inch to 6 inches in size to handle 1 to 500 gpm. For larger installations using nonpotable water, sand filters plus screens are recommended.

Filters and screens must be cleaned periodically by hand or by built-in backflushing if the drip system is to function properly. Depending on water quality and filter size, the cleaning is necessary weekly, twice a week, or twice a month. Once a month the clamp at the end of each lateral line should be released to flush out accumulated sediment.

Filter unit to keep debris from entering water flow. *Photo by Michael Jay*

Injectors

Injectors are used to apply fertilizer, algaecides, and other materials into the lines. Injectors are piston and powerrun, creating a pressure drop across an orifice or sucking material for treatment from a tank. The injector is attached to the main water line.

Pressure Regulators

Most drip systems require some pressure regulation—a brass or plastic mechanical pressure regulator is most often used. Pressures for different emitters vary from 2 or 3 to 30 or 40 psi. Pressure reducers slow the flow of water. Most municipalities pump water to hoses at pressures ranging from 50 to 90 psi. The drip system delivers water to plants at low pressures, at about 15 to 45 psi. Some preset regulators reduce 175 psi or lower pressures down to 20 or 30 psi (+ 10 percent) for flows of 2 to 16 gpm. A low-flow regulator (PR-20L) is for flows of 0.10 to 8 gpm. A combined valve and adjustable

A fertilizer unit can be attached to a drip system. Note pressure-reducer valve.   *Photo by Michael Jay*

pressure regulator can simplify installation by allowing the exact pressures desired. Look for these items at your plumbing dealer or in hardware stores.

Automatic Controls

The automatic watering devices now on the market make watering a garden seem miraculous. Unlike standard controls, these do not waste water by turning on the device when it is raining or cool. The devices irrigate the soil the moment that soil moisture falls below normal. These systems currently cost between $50 and $125. Three parts are common to most of these systems:

Controller This has one dial you set to determine how dry the soil must be before moisture starts and one dial to tell you how long to keep water on.

Moisture Sensor This is buried in the root zone of the plants; it signals the controller when the soil is dry.

Electric Valve This turns on water when signaled by the controller.

To convert a manual valve to a timer system, unscrew the on-off control and replace it with its electric counterpart or actuator.

Several manufacturers make these systems; check with local hardware stores or drip system suppliers.

Clocks

Special clocks provide timed water applications ranging from 5 minutes to 24 hours for any predetermined number of days. The clocks, which are powered by electric lines, batteries, or water, activate control valves that turn water on and off as needed.

Valves

The use of a main valve will allow you to shut off the entire system. Local codes may require a blackflow-prevention device. With a pressure vacuum breaker you can have separate valves downstream. Any atmospheric vacuum breakers you use have to be placed after each line valve; the breaker or the line valve has to be 12 inches higher than all piping downstream, or you may have to use a reduced-pressure backflow preventer.

Each line should have a manual or automatic valve. You should seriously consider automating the system because good drip practice requires daily or at least every-other-day watering to achieve even soil moisture. A Greenlawn 24-volt valve is recommended because it works on very low flow.

Adapters and Fittings

An adapter ties in to hose thread, and PVC (polyvinyl-chloride) slip sockets; the other end of the adapter is a compression fitting that slips over ½- or ¾-inch poly tubing. Polybutylene tubing requires special Kwic Loc fittings. Each end of the line should have an end plug with either an unscrewing cap or an automatic drain plug so that lines can be flushed.

Operation of the Drip System

After assembling the system on the surface, open all end caps. If the pressure regulator is adjustable, set it to OFF.

Above: Component parts—pipes and adapters. Below: Parts shown attached. *Photos by Michael Jay*

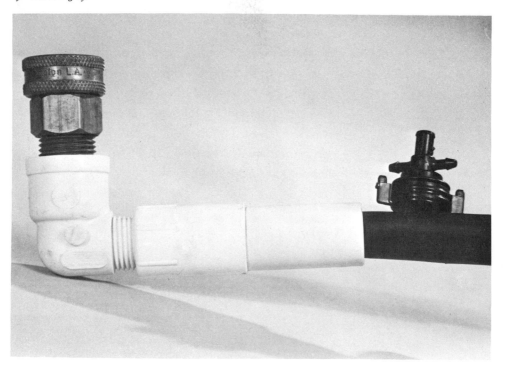

Turn on the water, gradually increasing the water to operating pressure, to flush all the lines thoroughly. Then turn off the water and secure the end caps.

Repressurize and examine all emitters to be sure none is clogged from dirt in the line. Flush emitters manually if necessary.

Operate your system at the lowest pressure (2 to 30 psi) that your elevation differential will allow. It takes 43 psi of pressure to raise water 100 feet in elevation. At the top of a hill allow at least 12 psi more for emitters to operate properly, or set them for 45 psi to overcome the elevation in terrain. When drip lines are set downhill they pick up pressure in the same proportion, so set pressure low when feeding from the top of a hill. By running drip lines level on the sides of hills you will prevent such pressure adjustments.

Other Drip Systems

Drip and Mist Watering System

In addition to Sub Terrain, there are several other major manufacturers of drip watering devices. Although most drip systems require a water-reducing valve to reduce city water pressure from 80 to 40 psi, a few systems can be connected directly to the water outlet. One of these is Drip and Mist Watering System of San Juan Capistrano, California. This company offers conventional drip emitters for above-ground installation, and also manufactures mist and sprinkler emitters. Here are their basic guidelines:

1) Prepare a sketch of the garden area to be watered. Mark all plants to be watered, and then choose the emitter required (see watering information in Table 4).

TABLE 4/WATER APPLICATION GUIDE (*Drip and Mist Mfg. Co.*)

Type of plant	Recommended watering method	Typical moisture application (minutes per day)		
		Hot and windy	Warm	Cool
Ground cover, flower beds, and small planter areas	Use a low-volume sprinkler every 4 feet, or use soaker tubing above or below ground every 12–15 inches (soaker has approximately 1-gallon flow per foot per hour).	15	10	5
Tropicals and ferns	Use mist sprayers from overhead or surface, or low-volume sprinklers or emitters on the surface as desired.	15	10	5
Vegetables	Use soaker tubing along garden row above or below ground; use 1½- or 4-gallon emitter for mound crops.	15	10	5
Small shrubs	One emitter per plant	15	10	5
6- to 10-foot trees	Four 4-gallon emitters on four sides at a point half the distance from the trunk to the outer foliage	15	10	5
10- to 18-foot trees	Four or more 4-gallon emitters	15	10	5

2) Add the total gallons required to water all plants, and then determine whether to use ⅜- or ½-inch tubing for your main water line. For up to 80 gallons use ⅜-inch tubing; for up to 240 gallons, use ½-inch line.

3) Put the main line at a convenient hose outlet. Measure the tubing to run the main line through the area where watering is needed.

4) Determine additional tubing requirements. Use T attachments in the main line to connect ½-, ⅜-, or ¼-inch branch lines to specific areas to be watered. Use ¼-inch branch or spur lines to reach plants far away.

5) Determine additional components needed (see components list, below).

6) Remember that the hose filter assembly is the first component to attach directly to the water hose or to the pressure reducer (if one is needed).

7) Tubing becomes more pliable and thus easier to lay out if it is left in the sun for a few hours prior to installing.

8) Check with local building and safety commissions or planning divisions for blackflow-prevention (antisiphon) valve requirements.

Reed Irrigation System
(Drip Eze)

Another home gardening drip system called Drip Eze, manufactured by Reed Irrigation System of Cajon, California, uses a pressure-relief valve connected to a faucet located in the area to be watered. A female adapter is threaded on the valve, and tubing is laid out along the area to be watered. Emitters are then attached with a clamp punch, pressed into the tubing hole, and hooked onto the tubing.

If you are watering one plant, remove the feeder T and put a feeder-tube nipple on the emitter. You can also scissor-cut the feeding tube to a desired length (if the emitter is not close enough to the plant) and attach one end into the feeder-tube nipple; place the other end at the plant. If two plants are to be watered from one emitter, scissor-cut the feeder tubing long enough to reach from the emitter T to the plant.

Once emitters are placed, you simply turn on the faucet and set the dial of the pressure-relief valve to the ON position. As the tubing fills with water, excess water will leak behind the dial of the pressure valve. When all the emitters are dripping, you turn the dial clockwise just until the water stops leaking. The system is now set to deliver 2 gph per emitter, with 15 psi of water pressure in the tubing. You can bury the system if you like, but you must be sure the dripping end of the feeder tubing or the dripping top of the emitter is above ground.

The watering chart for the Drip Eze system is in Table 5.

TABLE 5/WATER APPLICATION GUIDE (*Drip Eze*)

			Total watering hours per week		
Plant	*No. of emitters*	*Distance of emitters from plant or tree*	*Hot weather*	*Warm weather*	*Cool weather*
Ground cover	1 every 2 feet	At plant	12	6	3
Flower beds and vegetable gardens	1 with feeder 2 feeder tubes to plants	Less than 36 inches when using feeder tubing	12	6	3
Low shrubs	1	1 foot	12	6	3
10-foot trees	2	1½ feet	24	12	6
20-foot trees	4	2 feet	24	12	6
Larger trees	6	3 feet	24	12	6

Gro-Mor System

Finally, one should consider the Gro-Mor drip watering system. This employs a four-barrel flow-control valve having four outlets, with narrow grooves leading to each of the four holes. These grooves, in combination with the rubber valve, permit a fixed number of gallons of water per hour to pass through each hole. The Gro-Mor flow-control valve is designed to operate at normal domestic water pressures. An antisiphon device is also used.

The system is assembled as follows. Screw the antisiphon device onto the faucet you will use for watering. Attach the flow-control valve into the antisiphon device. Place a stainless steel O ring about ¼ inch over one end of the distribution tubing; place that end of the tubing over one of the outlets on the flow-control valve and secure it with the ring. Now lay out distribution tubing. Fold over the free end of the distribution tubing and insert it into a Gro-Mor end cap. Do this for each flow-control valve outlet. Next, cut microflow emitters (in this case, the tube) to the required lengths. With the insertion tool, punch one hole where you want an emitter. Insert emitters at least 2 inches into the tubing. The punched hole forms a tight seal between the emitter and the tubing. The system is now ready for operation and may be buried or left on the surface of the ground.

Gardens   Each microflow emitter accommodates an area approximately 18 to 20 inches in diameter. Plant rows should be about 9 to 12 inches apart; emitters should be placed at the same level. Place each length of distribution tubing between every other row, so each length waters two rows. Use 9-inch emitter tubing placed into distribution tubes at approximately 18- to 20-inch intervals, beginning about 9 inches from the plant rows. Push each tube emitter halfway into the larger tube. A garden watered in this manner requires up to 1 gallon per day for every 10 square feet.

Trees   Use one outlet of the flow-control valve for each tree. Run a piece of tubing to each tree, and encircle the trunk with it once. Insert four microflow emitters of uniform length at equally spaced points around the tree. Push the microflow emitters halfway into the distribution tube. Mature trees require about 30 gallons per day.

Parts or Components List

Here is a representative parts list from a manufacturer that will familiarize you with the various components of a drip system (generally for all systems):

Dual shut-off valve Fits faucet or hose end.

Hose-to-pipe adapter The hose-to-pipe adapter is required to adapt hose fittings to standard pipe threads. Use ¾ inch for most antisiphon valves and ½ inch to adapt to sprinkler risers. Not required for faucet or hose connections.

Hose filter assembly The hose filter assembly is installed directly onto the hose-to-pipe adapter or faucet. The 80 mesh stainless-steel screen slides out for easy cleaning.

Fertilizer/filter assembly Use for larger systems or to introduce any solid, water-soluble fertilizer into the system.

Screen washer Provides minimum filtration, so is for small systems only.

Flow regulator (hose shut-off) In-line shutoff for part of system or to control amount of flow.

Tubing connector Push tubing into fitting for permanent watertight fit. Female has swivel-hose fitting.

To adapt tubing to PVC, male fitting will solvent-weld into standard ½-inch PVC socket.

Reducing coupling ½ x ⅜ inch For joining ½-inch tubing to ⅜-inch tubing.

Repair coupling Cut tubing even and push in for repair.

L coupling For sharp corners in tubing.

Compression T or T adapter Push tubing in for permanent watertight fit. Use ⅜-inch adapter to convert one leg of ½-inch T to ⅜-inch tubing, use ½-inch adapter for ⅜-inch T conversion. (Requires PVC solvent.)

End cap Use on #5M tubing connector to end ⅜-inch or ½-inch tubing.

Emitter (variable flow) Insert directly into main line or at end of ¼-inch tubing. Tab color indicates flow rates. Line up bar on tab with two dots on emitter housing for full flow and one dot for approximately half flow—anywhere between is off. (Some may drip slightly when in the off position.)

Mist sprayer Insert directly into ⅜- or ½-inch main line or at end of ¼-inch tubing. Use 3 gallons for fine mist, 6 gallons for heavy mist.

Low-volume sprinkler head (15 gph) Flat trajectory full-circle sprinkler head with 4-foot diameter.

¼-inch single connector For joining ¼-inch line to ⅜-inch tubing. Also for splicing ¼-inch tubing.

¼-inch T connector For joining two ¼-inch lines to ⅜-inch or ½-inch tubing, or to form a T in ¼-inch tubing.

¼-inch L connector For sharp corners in ¼-inch tubing.

Hole plug Provides seal in ⅜- or ½-inch line when connectors are removed. Will seal end of ¼-inch line.

Comes in package of 6.

Tubing hole punch Used to punch holes in ⅜- or ½-inch poly tubing to insert emitter barb or ¼-inch connector barbs.

Nylon straps (8 inch) Self-locking cable ties to strap any size tubing in place. Trim off excess for smaller tubing.

Tubing mounting clips (⅛ inch) For stucco, masonry, or wood. Comes in package of 15.

Tubing mounting clips (¼ inch) For stucco, masonry, or wood. Comes in package of 15.

Tubing staples (#5) 1¼- and ½-inch for wood only. Come in package of 40. Same as electrical staples found in most hardware stores.

Tubing staples (#10) ⅜-inch for wood only. Come in package of 15.

Tubing mounting clips ⅜-inch for stucco, masonry, or wood. Come in package of 4.

½-, ⅜-, and ¼-inch polyethylene tubing Extremely high-quality flexible tubing that retains its resiliency after years of above- or below-ground use. Designed for commercial farming, grove, or orchard application to provide care-free service for up to 60 psi. Not designed for static pressure conditions.

⅛-inch polyethylene tubing Fits in end of emitter tab to extend the flow.

Backflow preventer (Antisiphon) Use in main line to prevent irrigation water from being siphoned back into water service in the event of pressure loss.

Special ¼-inch connector Hose thread to ¼-inch tubing; use on faucet or hose end to adapt ¼-inch tubing, or to connect ¼-inch tubing to sprinkler riser.

Whenever you are considering a watering setup, cost is of course a factor. The other factor is whether you will plan and install it yourself, call in a contractor, or consult with a landscape architect. Neither factor is a problem if approached intelligently, so let us first look at cost.

Cost

You can have a drip watering system for as little as $100, or it may cost you as much as thousands of dollars (for large acreage). Generally, for the average home garden of, say, 500 square feet (25 × 20 feet), a very good drip system can be installed for about $100. This does not mean that every plant will receive drip irrigation—some plants, such as ground covers, lawns, and many trees, may not need it. The cost may seem high at the outset, but little additional cost is involved once the systems are installed.

The drip system is as economical—if not more so—than a conventional sprinkler system. For my main garden, which is approximately 200 × 20 feet, a conventional sprinkler system was quoted by a plumbing contractor at $2500. I had a drip system installed for $1400. For my side garden, 40 × 20 feet, which is on a steep incline and terraced, the estimated cost of a sprinkler system (which would have done little good since the water would have run off) was $1500. A drip system installed on the fence ran about $800.

If you consider that a good 100-foot hose these days costs about $40, and you need three hoses to water a 20-by 20-foot garden, you can see that drip watering is not exorbitant. (You will cut your water bills tremendously over the years, every year.)

The choice of the system and the cost is also dictated by automatic or manual hardware and other accoutrements. The drip system can be modest in cost, or, if sophisticated with shutoff and release valves, much more expensive.

Do You Need Planning Help?

A landscape architect or a garden sprinkler company representative can of course lay out the pipe and grid plan for your garden. If you can afford these people, fine. If you cannot, do it yourself. All you need is what we previously outlined: a good sketch with existing plants. Then check out the plants to determine which ones really need a lot of water and which ones can get along on a little water. In this way you can space emitters intelligently.

All that is necessary is an intelligent investigation of your plants and your garden in order to proceed with the system that is best for your situation. If you have an average-size garden, by all means do it yourself. For larger areas you might want outside help. A consultation or two with a landscape architect is not that expensive; tell him or her immediately that you want only one or two discussions and that finished drawings may not be necessary. Inquire about fees. This advice also applies when consulting with garden / sprinkler companies. You can find suitable professional help through the Yellow Pages of your phonebook.

Maintenance

Any type of watering system requires maintenance. You should check emitters periodically to see if they are dispensing water properly, and you should inspect pipe to be sure it is intact. If hose-type emitters are clogged, rod them out by using a length of monofilament fishing line. If hardware-type emitters are clogged, flush them out. Check flow filter valves occasionally—remove screen and rubber discs and wash all parts thoroughly.

Drip systems should be flushed and cleaned annually by opening the end caps. And if you are not going to use the system for a long time, dismantle it and store the components in plastic bags. In anticipation of a freeze, always make sure that water is out of the flow-control valve and antisiphon device.

For your own convenience you might want to put the drip system on a clock valve (sold at hardware stores). Then set the clock so the garden is watered automatically. Most gardens require only one clock.

Always check with your local building and safety commission for backflow-preventer (antisiphon) valve requirements.

Drip Systems Suppliers

Many hardware stores carry drip watering kits and component parts for other systems. In addition, the following manufacturers will provide information and brochures pertaining to their products:

Drip and Mist Watering Systems
by Care-Free Irrigation Supplies, Inc.
P.O. Box 151
San Juan Capistrano, CA 92675

Sub Terrain Irrigation Co.
1534 East Edinger
Santa Ana, CA 92705

Reed Irrigation Systems
P.O. Box X
El Cajon, CA 92022

Gro-Mor
3156 East La Palma
Anaheim, CA 92806

6. Watering Potted Plants

NOW THAT HOUSEPLANTS are an important aspect of home decoration, I am often asked "When do I water my houseplants?" Again, it is not so much when you water but how you water. This is where drip irrigation can come to the aid of even the apartment gardener. The water-well container, introduced in about 1965 and refined thereafter, works on the same premise as a drip irrigation system: it supplies a little moisture over a long period of time. Other watering devices include wicks and water vials.

Drip Watering

With a drip watering kit, the emitter is placed in the pot itself. Plants are watered uniformly and with the proper amounts because water gets to the roots. All the guesswork of when to water is eliminated. Of course, for best results the plants must be arranged in fairly close proximity—that is, they must be in one area of, say, not more than 100 square feet.

Most people do group their plants, so the application of a drip system is ideal and it saves water as well. For about $25 you can water six 5- to 7-inch pots in your indoor garden.

Water-well Containers

These are double-section (one-piece) molded plant pots sold under various trade names. The lower pot holds the water reservoir, and the roots draw water from the top well only as needed through a porous stem-type attachment. In this manner there is no guesswork. The plant takes what it needs. You simply fill the reservoir about once every 3 weeks. Pots are available from 4- to 10-inch sizes; the larger containers cost about $30.

A commercial drip water-wick container; water is delivered to the plant slowly and steadily. Available for houseplants.

Self-watering tray

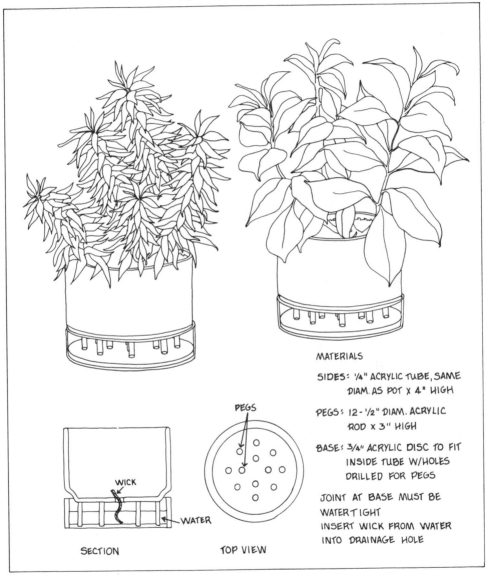

MATERIALS

SIDES: ¼" ACRYLIC TUBE, SAME
    DIAM. AS POT x 4" HIGH

PEGS: 12 - ½" DIAM. ACRYLIC
    ROD x 3" HIGH

BASE: ¾" ACRYLIC DISC TO FIT
    INSIDE TUBE W/HOLES
    DRILLED FOR PEGS

JOINT AT BASE MUST BE
WATERTIGHT
INSERT WICK FROM WATER
INTO DRAINAGE HOLE

PEGS

WICK

WATER

SECTION   TOP VIEW

Some pots employ a wick system. An ordinary candle wick runs from the reservoir to the plant soil. Again, capillary action furnishes the moisture to the plants, and the slow continuous supply of water benefits the plants.

Although the water-well containers or reservoirs work well for potted plants, they are even better for seeds. Seed-starting trays made of plastic have a water well. I have tried these seed containers and found that the seeds in them grew better and more quickly than in conventional trays.

Easy Wicking

You can make your own drip system watering container from fiberglass rope or woven wicks. Cut off a 3-inch piece of rope or wick and insert it through the drainage hole of a potted plant. Now put the pot on the gravel bed; place the other end of the wick in a can or bottle of water. When the soil starts to dry out, water will be drawn up the wick through capillary action and moisture will be supplied to the soil. The total cost of this system is about $1.

If you are repotting a plant and want to use a wick watering system, simply extend the wick about 1 inch into the soil and 2 to 3 inches out of the drainage hole. In a more sophisticated system you could hide the water reservoir and put wicks into several pots in a row. This would work, for example, in a windowbox arrangement. Just remember always to keep the water reservoir filled with water.

Water Vials / Bubblers

These simple watering devices generally operate on the same principle as wick watering except that the vial or plastic container holding the water is inserted on the top of the soil. When the soil becomes dry, the waterer automatically releases moisture in small amounts into the soil.

Patio Pots and Planters / Hanging Baskets

If you have plants on your patio or terrace, use drip watering to be sure they grow and grow. Connect a ⅜- or ½-inch line to the hose outlet and run the line up the posts or other vertical structures in the patio; then run ¼-inch tubing from the main line to the potted plants. Set a stake in the soil of the pot to hold the emitter. Mount mist sprayers overhead on beams or walls, or on fences, for steady misting. This system is especially good for plants like fuschias and impatiens. In protected areas, sprayers can be mounted up to 36 inches above the plants.

For hanging or wall-mounted basket plants, use one 3- or 6-gallon mister above the basket for 15 minutes each day. This should supply sufficient water, except in very dry, windy climates where 20 to 30 minutes of watering may be necessary. For patio pots and planters, use one ½- to 4-gallon emitter (depending on the size of the pot mounted) to drip into the soil for 15 minutes. If you

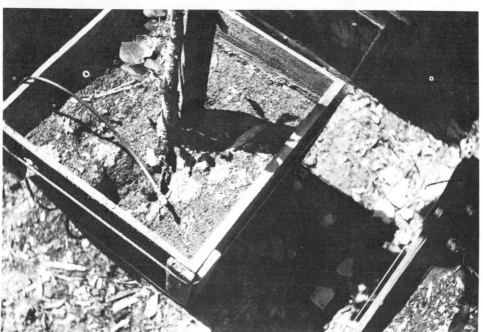

On the facing page, above: For container watering, an emitter is placed on the main line; a spur line is run directly into the soil to water the plant. *Photo courtesy Drip and Mist Watering Co.*

Below: The tree in a container is watered with emitter placed on a stake pushed into the soil; the spur line comes off the main line. *Photo courtesy Sub Terrain Irrigation Co.*

Here, shrubs in cans are being watered by the drip method. The main pipe runs along the top of the wall; emitters are placed above each plant and spur lines (two to a container) are run into the soil. *Photo courtesy Drip and Mist Watering Co.*

Pipes and lines are hidden below rafters to furnish water to hanging plants—another way to utilize drip watering. *Photo courtesy Drip and Mist Watering Co.*

On the facing page: The hanging baskets on the patio are being watered with a slow steady spray; note emitters at the bottom of the beam. *Photos courtesy Drip and Mist Watering Co.*

Patio drip system

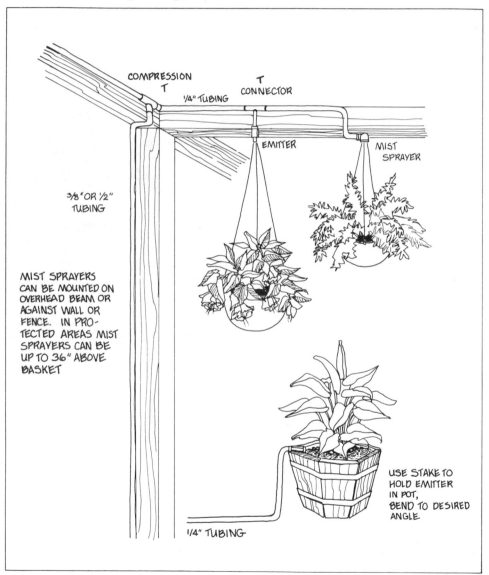

COMPRESSION T

1/4" TUBING

T CONNECTOR

EMITTER

MIST SPRAYER

3/8" OR 1/2" TUBING

MIST SPRAYERS CAN BE MOUNTED ON OVERHEAD BEAM OR AGAINST WALL OR FENCE. IN PRO-TECTED AREAS MIST SPRAYERS CAN BE UP TO 36" ABOVE BASKET

USE STAKE TO HOLD EMITTER IN POT, BEND TO DESIRED ANGLE

1/4" TUBING

elect to spray plants, use one 3-gallon mist sprayer above your pots. Installation takes an hour or so, but once done, that is it—you only have to turn on the water.

If there are no vertical posts on the patio or terrace, you can still use drip gardening; follow the same methods as for standard garden installation, but run ¼-inch line with an emitter on a stake into the soil for each plant.

7. The Future of Drip Irrigation

THE FUTURE OF drip system watering both for commercial crops and home use is bright indeed. With the increasing cost of water, any type of water-saving apparatus pays for itself in a short time. More important, if water becomes scarce—and we have factual information that it will—the drip watering concept may be the only intelligent way to make plants grow.

Home Usage

The drought of 1977 brought drip systems into the average home garden. Many people adapted soaker hoses, then more sophisticated drip systems as they became available, in an effort to save water and save their gardens. Even a small garden is a costly investment of time and money so any water-saving method of keeping plants alive became extremely popular.

Once the drought was over people did not return to sprinklers and hose watering because they had found the joys of using slow, steady watering: bigger and better plants and less work.

As the demand grew, manufacturers responded and converted commercial systems that would be suitable for small home gardens. Kits appeared, as mentioned, and many dealers started to carry component parts for do-it-yourselfers who wanted to install a drip system in their garden.

Most people, especially in California, Arizona, and other western states, discovered that drip watering made the difference between having a garden and not having one. Few people have the time to water their garden every day the conventional way, and in areas where there is little or no rain from April to November the drip system was, and is, the answer.

The future for home drip watering systems is very sunny; as more manufacturers respond to the demand, prices for apparatus become lower, and more sophisticated hardware is introduced and made available to the general public. And we hope this book as well contributes to the popularity of drip watering in home gardens.

Commercial Application

Water and plant life have always been a vital factor of urban life. Now, in an era of concern over ecology, and to create esthetic beauty, it is more important than ever before to establish "garden cities" and to reclaim useless land and make it useable. Oxygen-giving trees and shrubs and beautiful landscapes must be part of our future in the concrete worlds. And it is very possible to attain these dream cities with drip watering.

While the drip watering system is not a panacea for all city woes, it can go a long way in opening up land for use and establishing ideal settings for living.

Our freeways that link cities together are another area where drip watering plays an important role. Freeways and right-of-way medians can now foster growth despite steep banks. Special installations of drip systems have proven that plants can grow along freeways because there is sufficient water penetration for high-density plant growth with little runoff onto road surfaces.

For large installations—shopping malls and public parks—drip watering is again the answer. It is less costly than commercial watering over the long run, and saves water. Hosing plants with water is impractical, and sprinklers interfere with traffic. The area devoted to plants in malls and parks will increase once the drip watering concept is adopted. Such systems already exist in many public areas.

Drip watering can and should be used for slopes, especially on a large scale, such as highway bankings. A commercially made mat that is a matrix of paper and synthetic woven fiber could possibly have soaker tubing woven into the mats at intervals. Then the mat could be rolled out onto a slope, with the ends hooked up, and by using flow-control devices could effectively control water down a slope. This "paper" netting would be ideal for holding the moisture for seed germination. The possibility of an almost instantly planted and irrigated hillside with no airborne moisture is an exciting concept. Experiment continues in this area, and there is a definite chance that this drip watering mat system might someday come into use.

Food Production

In the area of food production drip watering has already been proven an efficient and practical way to grow more produce quickly.

The costs of fertilizers, labor, and water are rising as resources are depleted. Farmers everywhere must use the most efficient way of growing their crops. Drip watering systems have been proven as a way (sometimes the only way) to make land profitable. Systems furnish water to sugar cane fields in Hawaii, for tomatoes in the United Kingdom, oranges in Florida, vineyards in South Australia, asparagus and strawberries in California, vegetables in Abu Dhabi, stone fruits in Yugoslavia, and bananas in Central America. The results have been almost miraculous, with larger fruits and more yield per acre—a definite boon.

In the future it is likely that at least half the crops in the United States will be watered the drip way where feeding is controlled along with water. This is an exciting area of research and work continues on it daily.

Problems to Be Solved

It is important to establish a standardization of tubing sizes for drip watering systems. Bob Anthis of Drip and Mist Watering Systems of San Juan Capistrano, California, tells me that this is one of the major drawbacks in the industry. He stated that there are three sizes of nominal ½-inch tubing used in the industry at this time. This makes it difficult for an installer—let alone the homeowner—to extend or repair an existing system.

Another problem to be solved, according to Anthis, is the standardization of different pressure and flow rates. Currently there are systems from 2psi to 60 psi. Users generally do not know the difference, so when they try to hook up thin tubing to a high-pressure system, nothing works.

None of these problems is impossible to solve, and work goes on to make systems more efficient, less costly, and proven. Time will solve the problems—remember that drip watering is still a recent innovation, but a needed and very welcome one to keep our green world beautiful and alive.

Index